"AMERICAN SOCIETY FOR QUALITY - QIC"

DON'T STUB YOUR PINKIE™
ON THE SPACE BAR

OFFICE EMAILS
THAT REALLY CLICK

Other Telecom Titles
From Aegis Publishing Group

Telecom Business Opportunities
*The Entrepreneur's Guide to Making
Money in the Telecommunications
Revolution* by Steve Rosenbush
$24.95   1-890154-04-0

Winning Communications Strategies
*How Small Businesses Master Cutting-
Edge Technology to Stay Competitive,
Provide Better Service and Make More
Money* by Jeffrey Kagan
$14.95   0-9632790-8-4

How to Buy the Best Phone System
*Getting Maximum Value Without
Spending a Fortune*
by Sondra Liburd Jordan
$9.95   1-890154-06-7

Telecom Made Easy, 4th ed.
*Money-Saving, Profit-Building Solutions
for Home Businesses, Telecommuters and
Small Organizations* by June Langhoff
$19.95   1-890154-14-8

Phone Company Services
*Working Smarter with the Right Telecom
Tools* by June Langhoff
$9.95   1-890154-01-6

900 Know-How
*How to Succeed With Your Own 900
Number Business* by Robert Mastin
$19.95   0-9632790-3-3

**The Business Traveler's
Survival Guide**
*How to Get Work Done While on the
Road* by June Langhoff
$9.95   1-890154-03-2

**Getting the Most From Your Yellow
Pages Advertising**
Maximum Profits at Minimum Cost
by Barry Maher
$19.95   1-890154-05-9

1-800-Courtesy
*Connecting With a Winning Telephone
Image* by Terry Wildemann
$9.95   1-890154-07-5

Telecom & Networking Glossary
*Understanding Communications
Technology, 2nd ed.* by Robert Masin
$14.95   1-890154-19-9

Data Networking Made Easy
*The Small Business Guide to Getting
Wired for Success* by Karen Patten
$19.95   1-890154-15-6

**Strategic Marketing in
Telecommunications**
*How to Win Customers, Eliminate
Churn, and Increase Profits in the
Telecom Marketplace*
by Maureen Rhemann
$39.95   1-890154-17-2

Digital Convergence
*How the Merging of Computers,
Communications, and Multimedia Is
Transforming Our Lives* by Andy Covell
$14.95   1-890154-16-4

The Telecommuter's Advisor
Real World Solutions for Remote Workers
by June Langhoff
$14.95   1-890154-10-5

**The Telecommunication Relay
Service (TRS) Handbook**
*Empowering the Hearing and Speech
Impaired*
by Franklin H. Silverman, Ph.D.
$9.95   1-890154-08-3

The Cell Phone Handbook
*Everything You Wanted to Know About
Wireless Telephony (But Didn't Know
Who or What to Ask)* by Penelope Stetz
$14.95   1-890154-12-1

DON'T STUB YOUR PINKIE™
ON THE SPACE BAR

OFFICE EMAILS
THAT REALLY CLICK

MAUREEN CHASE
SANDY TRUPP

Aegis Publishing Group, Ltd.
796 Aquidneck Avenue
Newport, Rhode Island 02842
401-849-4200
www.aegisbooks.com

Aegis Publishing Group, Ltd.
796 Aquidneck Avenue
Newport, RI 02842

International Standard Book Number: 1-890154-18-0
Printed in the United States of America.

10 9 8 7 6 5 4 3 2 1

Cover design by Metro Graphics

Library of Congress Cataloging-in-Publication Data
Chase, Maureen.
    Office emails that really click : don't stub your pinkie on the space bar / by Maureen Chase, Sandy Trupp.
        p. cm.
    Includes index.
    ISBN 1-890154-18-0
    1. Electronic mail messages. 2. Letter writing. I. Trupp, Sandy.
II. Title.

HE7551 .C47 2000
651.7'9—dc21   00-061813

We dedicate our book to the two people with whom we communicate the most, in so many ways ... our husbands.

FOR ROLAND & PHIL

ACKNOWLEDGMENTS

Many people understood the necessity for *Office Emails That Really Click* before we even wrote it. We want to offer our thanks for their encouragement and understanding.

We are deeply grateful to Bob Mastin, our editor and publisher. How could we have been any luckier? He recognized our special idea and helped make it come to life. We are indebted to both Bob and Denise Lanoue at Aegis Publishing for copyediting. Thanks to The Roberts Group: Tony and Sherry Roberts, for typesetting, graphic design, copyediting, and indexing.

We are fortunate to have the strong support of Philip Berry, director of publisher relations at National Book Network, and we thank him for his many suggestions and great enthusiasm toward our book. Thanks also to Miriam Bass, Rich Freese, Michael Sullivan, Carole Juárez, and Marianne Bohr, who have trumpeted the uniqueness of our book and our publishing backgrounds to so many people.

We are grateful for our incredible president, Rick Frishman, of Planned Television Arts, a division of Ruder Finn. "The world's greatest publicist" is also our dear friend and a supporter of this project from the start. We thank Rick for bringing us together in 1996, and Myra Peabody Gossens and Deborah Kohan for helping us find our way to PTA. We are indebted to David Hahn, David Thalberg, Hillary Rivman, Margaret McAllister, and John Brussel for their moral support, good humor, and constant emails. Thanks to our precious friend, Roz Safrin, who knows people better than anyone else. A special thanks to the great Ruder Finn Washington, DC team. We thank Amy Stelzner and Melissa Raddatz for their enthusiasm about our ideas, and for Amy's horror stories. Many thanks to our executive trainees and interns who have been part of the PTA team.

A warm thank you to Kathy and John Trupp of Metro Graphics for their expertise in design and for making our book cover and Web site (http://www.dontstubyourpinkie. com/) as cool as they are.

Maureen's Acknowledgments:

My wish is that our small contribution to communication will make the lives of working people a little bit easier. I hope this book helps people around the world "click" better.

Thank you to Torsten Chase for his expert knowledge in all things email. You are going places! I am indebted to Torsten for looking over the technical aspects of the book and to Kathleen Quirk for her assistance.

Thanks to the Ruder Finn team in New York and Washington for allowing me to create exciting ideas and call it "work." What a living. Thank you to our many clients and authors who motivated me to reach for the stars.

Thanks to Scott Major of Cleary & Komen, LLP. I am grateful for your expertise in intellectual property and all of the work you have put into our trademark.

I smile when I think of the great email stories contributed by my friends: Eileen and Kevin Brown, Kirstie Crawford, Pamela Giambo, Stephanie Graby, Kathy

Mekjian, Giselle Valera, and Jagruti Vaghasia. Thank you! I honor in these acknowledgments my professors and teachers throughout my life who have fostered creativity, encouraged curiosity, and in many cases, inspired perseverance: Judy Aimone, Jeff Barnett, Alex Brown, Gwyn Campbell, Melissa Cox, Peter Cronin, Burr Datz, Bob de Maria, Josephine Digan, Leonore Freeman, Sid Friedenberg, Lou Hodges, Farris Hotchkiss, John Jennings, George Kempfe, Bob Lampf, Gail Lighthype, Ron MacDonald, Ed McInroy, James Ransegnola, George Ray, Carleton Rehr, Dick Sessoms, Hampden Smith, Ed Yoder, and especially Brian Richardson for his insights about email communication.

I am grateful to my partner in crime, Sandy Trupp, for the exciting times we have shared, especially while writing our book. We did it!

I am fortunate to have the generosity and kindness of a loving family behind me. Thank you to my Chase parents and to Judy Gideon for their interest in the project. And thank you to my Levey family: Mom, Dad, Patti, Kathleen, Alison, Conor, and Brian (our true "star"), who provided daily doses of encouragement. Thanks to each of them for reading and commenting on our book as it evolved, and for inspiring me every day for the past 29 years. I am grateful to my Uncle Ray who is still lighting the way.

I feel gratitude beyond measure for my husband, Roland, for his editorial skills, gentle encouragement, and constant faith in me. Vielen dank, mein Lieber.

Sandy's Acknowledgments:

When we were kids, my brother, Wilfred Krause, and I used to communicate with "walkie-talkies," which he would make out of tin cans and string. Today I'm sending him emails.

We are fortunate to have had parents who encouraged us to go for it.

Over the years, I have represented hundreds of authors and have learned so much from all of them. Thank you to all of you. Now that I am an author, it does feel exciting to have co-written this book.

I would like to express my gratitude to my family: Becky, Buddy, John, Kathy, Zachary, Amy, Julian, and Sophia. Your enthusiasm for this book is golden. I have so many friends in book publishing who are out there still "Getting Caught Reading." But they are emailing with glee! A big thank you goes out to all of them, especially to the A Team at the original Acropolis Books under the leadership of Al Hackl.

To my dear friend Kathleen Hughes, publisher of IPM and Capital Books, thank you for insisting that we should get computerized! You're the quiz guru and your creativity has been an inspiration.

Thanks also to Lisa Shenkle and Ray Stubbs, both masters at sending and receiving communications, and to Gail Scott for good advice and emails that dance!

A special thank you to Daphne Harden, who is destined for the long-term friendship category and my newest email buddy. Now that she's online, email will rock (in a jazzy way).

It was so much fun to conceive and write this book with Maureen Chase. We have an amazingly strong friendship that keeps on clicking. My husband Phil always encouraged me to keep writing. He is full of ideas and stories, even marketing tips. But his strongest contribution is the nonverbal communication that we share together.

Contents

INTRODUCTION

Stop the madness before it proliferates! People spend too much time on electronic mail today to ignore the need for a guidebook. Electronic mail has become a critical and ubiquitous business tool, one that is important enough to have its own set of rules and standards. That's why we wrote this book.

Office Emails That Really Click will help you avoid common email mistakes, giving you the guidance and confidence you need to draft the most appropriate message for any occasion.

Before we go any further, though, we need to agree on how to refer to the shortened version of the term "electronic mail." Electronic mail is commonly referred to as E-mail, Email, e-mail, or email. We prefer "email" ("Email" at the beginning of a sentence). The trend is to drop the hyphen.

We love email and think it is a wonderful form of communication. But we also believe that people should not let the need for expedience interfere with the rules of English grammar and business protocol. In fact, we have interspersed throughout this book numerous grammatical tips in helpful sidebars.

This book also will give you a good model of what emails in the workplace should look like. *Office Emails That Really Click* outlines a complete and standard format for emails. We incorporate new ideas and trends in email along with well-respected guidelines for excellent communication. This book covers:

Business Protocol
→ You would like to thank a colleague for taking you to lunch. Is an emailed thank you note acceptable?

Sticky Situations
→ A fellow staff member sends you a risqué joke via email. What do you do?

Time Issues
→ Three hundred emails are waiting for you when you return from vacation. How do you sort through them all?

Spreading Good News
→ What is the appropriate format for announcing a promotion via email?

Spreading Bad News
→ You need to contact your nationwide staff regarding a memorial service for a colleague. What do you say in your email?

Personal Emails
→ You would like to ask your office staff out to a happy hour. What is the best wording for your email?

We have the answers to all of these questions and more. There is no need to obsess over what to say in your emails and how to say it. With this handy reference, you will never stub your pinkie on the space bar again!

After speaking with clients, colleagues, and friends, we have found there is a need and demand for a book about sending and receiving successful emails. In most offices today, there is no formal training session that covers the use of email. Between us, your authors, we handle (both send and receive) more than 500 emails per day. We are communications experts who are plugged into the world of business emails. We know what works—from experience. And, we advise our clients, who range from celebrities to corporate executives to politicians, on effective communication.

Office Emails That Really Click is for everyone in the workplace who uses email or would like to use email. We must ensure the preservation of our written language for a future that will rely heavily on email communication. And if you think you learned everything you need to know in kindergarten, think again—email wasn't even invented then.

Our main purpose in writing this book is to make life easier for email users, to raise questions about email, to provide some answers through easy-to-follow guidelines, and to make using email enjoyable. Our ultimate goal is to encourage each email user to use his or her "voice" in emails. With email rapidly becoming a primary means of business communication, the voice you convey in business emails—professional and concise or sloppy and disorganized—makes a lasting impression on important business contacts. Your emails reflect who you are.

We hope you have fun reading our book. And here's to sending successful emails that really "click."

Your friends,
Maureen and Sandy

CHAPTER 1

THE ELECTRONIC MAIL QUOTIENT QUIZ

No good book should begin without a quiz! The following questions will test your Electronic Mail Quotient or (EMQ) level.

The EMQ Quiz

1. **When you receive an email message that solicits a response, at what point is it appropriate to reply?**

   a) That same day—I hate to keep people waiting.

   b) Within a week.

   c) Do I have to reply?

2. **How often do you forward emails?**

   a) Only if it's an important message, such as a computer virus warning.

   b) Sometimes—there are some pretty funny jokes out there.

   c) All day long—I love all of those chain letters making the email circuit.

3. **Suppose you receive a "joke" email that you think is funny. To how many people might you forward it?**

   a) One person.

   b) Five to 10 people.

   c) Everyone in the free world.

4. **Have you ever been guilty of spamming?**

   a) No.

   b) Yes.

   c) What is spamming?

5. **When you send emails, do you usually use a subject header?**

   a) Yes, of course, I label all of my emails.

   b) No, why should I?

   c) What is a subject header?

6. **How often do you check your email?**

   a) Every five minutes—I can't wait any longer.

   b) Once or twice per day.

   c) Never—do I even have email?

7. **When you compose emails, do you usually use a greeting such as "Hello, Kathy"?**

   a) Yes.

   b) It depends.

   c) No, they know who they are.

8. **Do you spell check your emails?**

   a) Yes.

   b) No.

   c) Is that possible?

9. **How do you sign, or close, your emails?**

   a) With my full name or initials.

   b) With my nickname from college.

   c) I don't sign my emails. People should know who the sender is.

10. **Do you ever fulfill certain business obligations, such as thanking someone for a gift or sending out company party invitations, through email?**

   a) Often.

   b) Sometimes—it depends on the situation.

   c) Never—email is not the right forum.

11. **Is it okay to write emails in all capital letters, or even in all lowercase letters?**

   a) Never, unless you are intending to shout or whisper, respectively, at someone!

   b) Sometimes.

   c) Always, because it's much easier.

TRACK YOUR EMQ

The results are in. If most or all of your answers were…

A – You are "EMAIL LITERATE"
Congratulations! Look through *Office Emails That Really Click* to perfect your skills.

B – You are "EMAIL FRIENDLY"
Not bad! You are getting there. Take a look through *Office Emails That Really Click* and brush up on your email skills.

C – You need "HELP!"
It's okay. You can learn the tricks of the trade from *Office Emails That Really Click* and soon be clicking with the best of them.

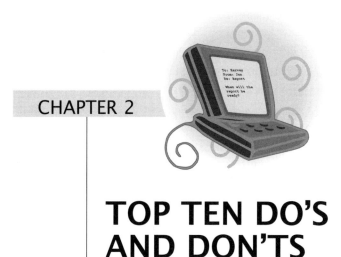

CHAPTER 2

TOP TEN DO'S AND DON'TS

Taking Your EMQ Skills to the Next Level

Do you have virtual seizures when you arrive at work and discover you have 375 unread emails, not to mention mountains of other work for the day? (We won't begin to touch on voice-mail messages.) How do you sort through all of those emails? How many email attachments have you gotten that may be infected with a computer virus? Do you need to use subject headers?

Well, there are rules for email communication, one of which is not to send too many emails to your colleagues, especially if they are nothing but unnecessary jokes or so-licitations. People don't have the time to sort through count-less "junk" emails per week. So be a responsible emailer and do your part to clean up the email pipeline; trash the junk emails.

In the following pages, we created the top 10 do's and don'ts for the most common email scenarios, based on research and interviews with experts and colleagues in business and commu-nications arenas. We asked people what their biggest peeves or questions were about email usage. Some of our do's and don'ts stem from the most common email complaints. Maybe they look familiar to you. Here are a few:

"I receive more than 100 emails per day. I wish people would stop to think about what they are sending before they press the SEND button on their computers."

"I would like to know what emails are urgent. People ought to write: URGENT, NEEDS IMMEDIATE ATTEN-TION, or REPLY WITHIN 24 HOURS on the subject line of an email. With the multitude of emails I receive, I need to know which ones require immediate action."

"Why do people send these lengthy emails? I wish they would just sum things up in a few lines, short and sweet."

"I would like to be taken off of my colleague's mailing list. Is there a polite way of saying 'please take me off of your mailing list'?"

"How do I get rid of cling-ons? You know, those people you meet once at a function, give them your email address, and they won't stop emailing you jokes. How do I get out of it?"

"When is it okay to end an email conversation? If I say 'thanks' or 'great job', and they respond 'you're welcome', do I need to say 'no problem'? Where does it end?"

Let's see if we can help sort it out for you in the inimitable style of David Letterman. We will start with the DON'TS. Don't worry—for every "don't" we have a corresponding "do" in the following lists.

TOP TEN DON'TS

10. DON'T send unnecessary mass emails. This includes forwarding unsolicited emails—such as jokes or chain letters, general messages, and advertising— to a long list of your coworkers.

9. DON'T send emails without greetings or closings.

8. DON'T send emails without subject headers, or with improperly denoted headers.

7. DON'T send urgent emails without labeling them as such; and don't assume the receiver has received your email—follow up. Don't label emails as urgent that aren't.

6. DON'T send private or confidential information over email.

5. DON'T spam. Just don't do it, and don't reply to spammers.

4. DON'T ignore incoming emails by not responding (unless they're spam).

3. DON'T use poor spelling and/or grammar in emails.

2. DON'T use all CAPITAL or all lowercase letters in email, and don't use an extremely small font so that people can hardly read what you are writing.

1. DON'T be a victim of the emotionless email.

TOP TEN DO'S

10. DO ask permission of your colleagues if they would like to be included in mass email lists, for jokes, chain letters, etc.

9. DO use proper greetings and closings in all of your emails.

8. DO use subject headers in all of your emails so that the recipient can quickly reference your incoming email and know what it is about.

7. DO label urgent emails, and only urgent emails, as such in the subject header; and always follow up with a phone call.

6. DO remember that no email is sacred. Be careful when sending private or confidential information in emails.

5. DO be considerate when sending unsolicited emails.

4. DO reply to emails that solicit a response, or even emails you think should be acknowledged.

3. DO remember to check your spelling and grammar.

2. DO reserve caps for when you want to convey a loud or shouting message. Use all lowercase if you are conveying a whisper in your email. Use at least a 10-point font size.

1. DO let your "voice" be heard in your emails.

In the following pages, we'll devote one chapter to each of the 10 "don'ts" and its corresponding "do."

CHAPTER 3

MASS EMAILS

#10: DON'T *send unnecessary mass emails. This includes forwarding unsolicited emails—such as jokes or chain letters, general messages, and advertising—to a long list of your coworkers.*

Having to wade through a seemingly endless maze of forwards is on everyone's email pet peeve list. Maybe some of these emails seem all too familiar to you.

IN SEARCH OF...THE EMAIL

To: JoJo Reese
From: Fred Franklin
Re: FWD: FWD: FWD: FWD: FWD: FWD: FWD:
FWD: FWD: FWD: FWD: FWD: FWD: FWD: FWD:
FWD: FWD: FWD: FWD: FWD: FWD: FWD: FWD:
FWD: FWD: FWD: FWD: FWD: FWD: FWD: FWD:
FWD: FWD: FWD: FWD: FWD: FWD: FWD: FWD:
FWD: FWD: FWD: FWD: FWD: FWD: FWD: FWD:
FWD: FWD: FWD: FWD: FWD: FWD: FWD: FWD:
FWD: FWD: FWD: FWD: FWD: FWD: FWD: FWD:
FWD: FWD: FWD: FWD: FWD: FWD: FWD: FWD:
FWD: FWD: FWD: FWD: FWD: FWD: FWD: FWD:
Funny stuff

To: Bob Reynolds, Anna Rodriguez, Jane
Goody, Edythe Burrows, Marylou Osterberg,
Buddy Jones, Jackie Sussex, Sammy Jacobitz,
Janine Ryan, Rhonda Paige, Ben Rosenblatt,
Amy Packard, Danny Falcone, etc.

Thought this was hilarious!

To: Jack Richardson, Paul Ruby, Amy Silocon,
Ruby Johnson, Robert Fischer, Annette
Rumble, Rebecca Gonzales, Allen Drew, Gil
Biddle, George Rizzo, Hampden Cox, etc.

What a hoot!

To: Jerome Seery, Betty Mullin, Boots
Johnson, Alice Washington, Ruth Johns, Jenny
McGuirkin, David Caballero, Marcia Robinson,
Kathleen Helen, etc.
And so on...

(More forwarded names continue down to the end of the page.)

A mother took her three-year-old daughter to church for the first time. The church lights were lowered, and then the choir came down the aisle, carrying lighted candles. All was quiet until the little one started to sing in a loud voice: "Happy Birthday to You!"

After minutes of scrolling down the email, finally, you find the joke. With all of that build-up, you thought it at least would be funny! It is not, like so many other jokes you receive.

JOKE OF THE DAY

To: Entire Global Office
From: Rosemary Davis
Re: Joke of the day

Finding one of her students making faces at others on the playground, Mrs. Smith stopped to gently reprimand the child. Smiling sweetly the Sunday school teacher said, "Bobby, when I was a child I was told that if I made ugly faces, my face would freeze and stay like that." Bobby looked up and said, "Well, you can't say you weren't warned."

Should I be laughing? And, why is this intelligent colleague of mine sending daily jokes? I don't really want them.

THE GRATUITOUS SEX JOKES

To: Jane Quirk, Joe Bishkin, Lani Raddatz, John Williams, Randall Rockett, Kristin Brown, Claire Cully, Mei Tierney, Sue Cifelli
From: Jack Sparks
Re: Great sex joke!

There once was a girl from Brisbane...

Uh oh. I know where this is going. Risqué jokes certainly can be funny, but will the office manager agree? Some jokes don't belong in the workplace—much less in workplace communication.

THE DIRTY, ROTTEN FORWARD

To: Jennifer Choice, Rayburn James, Sydney Octavius, Rick French, Selma Louise, Ben Griffith, Patti Annie
From: Lucretia Jevne
Re: FWD: FWD: FWD: FWD: FWD: FWD: FWD:
FWD: FWD: FWD: FWD: FWD: FWD: FWD:
FWD: FWD: FWD: FWD: FWD: FWD: FWD:
FWD: FWD: FWD: FWD: FWD: FWD: FWD:
FWD: FWD: FWD: FWD: FWD: FWD: FWD:
FWD: FWD: FWD: FWD: FWD: FWD: FWD:
FWD: FWD: FWD: FWD: FWD: FWD: FWD:
FWD: FWD: FWD: FWD: FWD: FYI

Ha! Made ya look!

Your oh-so-clever colleague has found another ingenious way to waste his own company time and yours, too!

PLEASE OPEN THIS ATTACHED GAME

To: Entire Office
From: Wendy Finelli
Re: FWD: This is cool!

> Bunny says, "The annual Easter Egg hunt is back!" Click open right here to search for the eggs with Bunny. There are six colored eggs in all, symbolizing the colors of a rainbow. When you find all six, you will see a big surprise!

Hey, gang! This attached game takes several minutes to download, the exact time varying depending on the system resources. Then figure an average of five minutes to play the game. These games, while fun, tie up network resources. Plus, your productivity will plummet. Delete immediately!

I work for a publisher of art books and my colleagues and I often refer to cultural movements and styles in our emails. Do I capitalize the names of the movements?

Capitalize if the word is derived from a proper noun. For example: impressionism is lowercase, but Gothic is capitalized.

NOBODY'S HOME

To: Everyone You Know
From: Chantal Granier
Re: Cool opportunity

To Everyone!

My sister, Nancy, is going to Paris this summer and would like me to spread the word about her sublet opportunity. The apartment is a brownstone in the Upper East Side. It has two bedrooms, one bathroom, pretty pink wallpaper, a garbage disposal, friendly neighbors, and a dog named Fluffy. The neighbors are great, and there are lots of fun hall parties every Friday night.

The rent will be $2,500 per month, not including utilities.

Please call Nancy at 212-555-1234 for more information.

Thanks!

I live with my family of four in Westport, Connecticut. I can't be bothered with these emails!

?

How do I abbreviate the words inch, foot, and yard?

The correct abbreviations are: in. or " (inch), ft. or ' (foot), and yd. (yard).

IT WAS BAD THE FIRST TIME AROUND

To: Heather, JB, Kate
From: Anna Lise Friz
Re: FWD: FWD: FWD: FWD: Dumb blond jokes

When the blond heard that 90 percent of all crimes happened around the home, she moved.

Well, it was a little funny. But now that I have received it five times in two days from different friends, I don't want to see it ever again.

YOUR STAMP'S ON THIS ONE!

To: Everyone
From: Janie
Re: Help

Does anyone have a stamp?

Or a stapler? Or some tape? Then a litany of emails follow, such as "I have three stamps," or "I had a few yesterday.... sorry!" or "I have a whole book, but I will charge you interest." Shouldn't you be sending this to just a select group of colleagues? Do you really want your president to know you are out of stamps?

DO IT OR DIE

To: You and Everyone Else in the Office
From: Colleague
Re: Re: Re: Re: The Good Witch story

A little girl fell off of her bicycle and hit her head on the ground. She was momentarily unconscious. During those moments she was out, the Good Witch of the Southwest appeared before her, in a vision. The Good Witch told her to appreciate all of the good things life had to offer. The girl said, "Like my bike? Like my parents?" The Good Witch said yes and told her to tell everyone she knew about this wonderful message when she woke up. She did, and the good news gave her family much joy. Life is a wonderful and precious gift!

SEND THIS TO FIVE THOUSAND PEOPLE YOU KNOW BY FRIDAY OR BE VISITED BY THE BAD WITCH OF THE NORTHEAST. SHE IS VERY REAL. IF YOU SEND IT, THEN GOOD THINGS WILL COME TO YOU IN LIFE.

I am tired of being threatened. And I have heard enough cornball stories like this to last several lifetimes. If a family member sends it to me, that's one thing. But when it comes from the managing partner? Hey, colleague, make like a witch and take off.

> **#10: DO** *ask permission of your colleagues if they would like to be included in mass email lists, for jokes, chain letters, etc.*

E-Guidelines For Mass Emails

Don't you dislike getting emails with a long list of names and forwards? It is up to the sender to ask permission to send these. When sending a mass email, please send it to your list through the blind copy or mailing list method, explained below. You wouldn't want your email address forwarded to strangers, would you? (See also e-guidelines in chapter 8 on spamming.)

Remember to create and use address lists with care. When sending out a mass email, keep your recipients' email addresses private by using the blind copy option (BCC), which is available in many email systems (such as Lotus Notes) right in the header. Not everyone, especially clients, like their emails to be distributed to others.

TIP: To use the BCC option, leave the "To" and "CC" spaces blank. Insert your name in the "From" section. Under "BCC," insert your list of recipients. The recipient will receive, in most systems, an email in which your name is listed in both the "To" and "From" spaces. The recipient's name won't even appear on the email at all. And, the recipient won't know who else has received this email.

If the BCC option is not available on your system, talk with your system administrator. Some systems allow you to set up the BCC option in other ways. For instance, you can set up mailing lists (sometimes called listservs). The idea is to accumulate specific email addresses in the list, and then name it, for instance, "Accounting Department." When sending an email to the addresses on this list (members of the accounting department, for example), you would insert that list's name (Accounting Department) in the "To" section of your email. Your recipients will see only the title (Accounting Department) in the address box, and not all of their names.

DID YOU GET THE JOKE?

To: Entire Office
From: Amy Price
Re: Joke list

Hi everyone,

Would you like to be on my joke-of-the-day list? It will give you a lot of giggles during the day that might be helpful to your overall well-being and work productivity. Please let me know by tomorrow morning. I will not send you anything unless I hear from you.

Thanks,
Amy

Here's a chance to be free of any bad jokes. Unless you can't resist.

AN OFFER YOU CAN REFUSE

To: Tracey
From: Lark
Re: Great offers

Hi Tracey,

I am compiling a special list to send messages about great offers for theater tickets, basketball games, etc. to the office staff. Would you like to be included on it? Please let me know by Tuesday morning.

Thanks,
Lark

This email gives people the chance to just say no, or to have the option of being included on that list.

What exactly is a typo?

"Typo" is an abbreviation for typographical error. Also called printer's error (PE) or misprint. The misprint does not refer to a writer's error, but to the printer's error or PE. For example: "Hte" instead of "the" is a typo.

A ROSE BY ANY OTHER NAME

To: Sheila
From: John
Re: Something interesting

Hi Sheila,

Please let me know if you would like me to forward you emails that I have received from other companies. These emails have a long list of forwards and I know that can be time-consuming and annoying, but believe me, they are worthwhile.

Thanks,
John

This may have information that you would want, and it is written in a thoughtful manner.

Can I use all capital letters in my emails? I want to make sure the recipient can clearly read my message.

Please, no. All caps makes your message more difficult—not easier—to read. Do not use all capital letters unless you must. In e-speak, capital letters are as good as shouting at your reader. Unless you would like to yell at your recipient, try to avoid writing emails in all capital letters. See chapter 11.

EDITORIAL WOES

To: Emma
From: James
Re: Fiscal report

Hi there!

Attached is my annual fiscal report. Can you proof it?

Thanks,
James

The reply follows:

PLAYING IT SAFE

From: Emma

James,

Would you mind printing out a copy and sending it to me overnight? My system administrator has asked me not to download large documents. I remember that last year's report was 120 pages, so would you mind?

Thank you,
Emma

Can I use contractions?

If you are writing a formal email, do without the contractions. In less formal emails, contractions are frequently used.

Remember when your mother told you not to send chain letters? And you said, "But, Mom, if I don't send this to 10 people, I will have seven years of bad luck! All the kids at school are doing it. I'll be the only one..." Well, you were not the only one then to break the cycle, and you won't be today. Just because all of the "big kids" at work or elsewhere are sending mass emails doesn't mean you have to do it, too.

If marketing is your game, however, you rely on email address lists and what email can do for you. When you do send messages to email lists, remember to be courteous, get to the point, and always give recipients an "out" option, so that they may remove themselves from your list. You could include the following in your email:

> "If you do not wish to be included in this mailing list, please email getmeouttahere@youremailaddress.com."

Privacy is the policy. As often as you can, blind copy your group emails to the recipients. You will make a lasting impression.

CHAPTER 4

GREETINGS AND CLOSINGS IN EMAILS

#9: DON'T *send emails without greetings or closings.*

Since we're creating a new voice with email, who wants to be anonymous? Always have a greeting and closing for every email you send. It is simply a courtesy. Not only that, you want the recipient to have a somewhat lasting reminder of you.

It takes 30 seconds to make a face-to-face first impression, but it only takes two words to sign off with a closing that is remembered. And you certainly don't want to be confused with someone else! Here are some pitfalls to avoid:

THE "WHO IS THIS PERSON?" EMAIL

To: Bob Lang
From: jrs56v@email.com
Re: Lunch

When would you like to have lunch? I'm free all next week.

I can't remember whose address this is. Who is this person? Jrs56v? A colleague? An agent? A client? The unidentifiable emailer also uses an inconsiderate tone that some recipients may take offense at and refuse to respond to.

THE COMMANDMENT EMAIL

To: Jason
From: Ramona
Re: Staff meeting

We will have a special staff meeting today at 11 a.m. in the large conference room. Bring all client information.

Sounds like a command, doesn't it?

"WHO'S THE BOSS?" EMAIL

To: The Boss
From: Staff member
Re: Gone

I'm out at 3 p.m. today.

Wouldn't you want to sound more polished than this when communicating with your boss?

FACE OFF

Face-to-face impersonal communications

To: Jeffrey Willis
From: Arnold White
Re: Lunch

When do you want to go to lunch?

Since this is a question between two people, why isn't there more personal attention given to this email?

I would like to send a message via email to three of my colleagues. May I send the message in one email to all three? If so, in my greeting, do I address them each by name, or can I say, "Hi All!"?

You may send the same message to all three, in one email. You do not have to address each person by name in the greeting if there are more than two names.

> **#9: DO** *use proper greetings and closings in all of your emails.*

E-Guidelines For Greetings And Closings

Would you ever call a client or colleague and not greet them with a salutation such as "Hi," "Hello," "Do you have a minute?" or "What's happening?" Would you call them up and, without greeting them or identifying yourself, simply say: "Can you get me a copy of the Hay-Adams report?" Like oral and written communications, emails should have greetings and closings, too. Address the recipient with a greeting, such as "Hello Rita." Sign off the email with a closing and your name, or your initials, such as "Thanks again, MC." Emails with no salutations or closings, but only the body of a letter, can come across as somewhat terse.

Some email programs have an auto signature feature that automatically provides your name and other details you choose to be included in the signature at the bottom of each email that you send. Include your address and phone number in the auto signature, too, in case the recipient has questions and would like to get in touch with you another way. If

I am writing a formal email to two gentlemen. What is the plural of Mr.?

The plural of Mr. is Messrs.

you use an auto signature, we still recommend that you sign your name. Would you send a letter with your name and title at the bottom, without your signature above? Some people do, but we find this highly impersonal.

Exceptions

→ **Acknowledgment emails:** When you receive an email that doesn't solicit a response but is more of an FYI email, do you respond? The answer is *yes*. You can email back a quick, "Thanks." You can waive the greetings and closings rule for the quick acknowledgment. If you don't acknowledge such an email, the sender, without a sophisticated email tracking system, might not know you received the email at all. The sender could actually write at the bottom of his or her email "acknowledgment appreciated" to track whether or not the email was received.

→ **Lengthy email conversations:** When you are emailing back and forth to someone you know well, you don't have to address him or her in each and every email with proper greetings and closings. Sometimes an email conversation about a certain issue could go back and forth several times. After each email participant writes his or her first email/response, the following exchanges do not necessarily need greetings and closings.

→ **Instant messages:** Some systems, such as America Online (AOL), have the instant message feature, which allows emailers to talk back and forth *live*. You don't need greetings or closings in these emails either. The urgent and instant nature of this feature precludes greetings and closings guidelines.

A WELL-ADDRESSED REQUEST

To: The Staff
From: Caitlin
Re: Time well spent

To All Charitable-Minded People,

For those of you who signed up for the Big Five Tournament in support of the homeless, your pledge forms have arrived. When you have a chance, please stop by my office to pick them up.

Thank you,
Caitlin

This cheerful email is bound to make people smile.

Is the word "everyone" singular or plural?

Singular. The pronouns used to refer to everyone are "his" or "her." The verb is also singular. For example: Everyone is going to want his or her own Web site by the year 2002.

WE'RE ALL PROFESSIONALS

To: The Staff
From: Georgie
Re: Staff meeting

Good Morning Everyone,

We will be having a special staff meeting this afternoon at 3:00 in the large conference room. Please let me know if you will be attending.

Have a great day,
Georgie

This is clear and direct and has a nice touch.

HAPPY TALK

To: Everyone
From: Betty
Subject: Promotion

Hi to All,

I really appreciate the kind words of congratulations from all of you. Thank you for thinking of me.

All the best,
Betty

Proper greetings are always appreciated.

HE'S GIVING YOU HIS NUMBER

To: All
From: Patrick
Subject: Secret files

To All,

This is an important message. Please do not leave home telephone numbers on top of the filing cabinet. It is extremely important to put all files in the file cabinet. We will have a special meeting about this soon.

Sincerely,
Patrick

Many of my colleagues are Spanish, as we have an office in Madrid. I have been told that in Spain, a person takes his father's last name and then his mother's, in that order. When addressing such a colleague in an email, do I use both names, just the first, or just the second? Sometimes, the two names are also separated by the letter "y." Do I include that, too?

Using both names is acceptable. For example: Julia Olmos Miranda or Julia Olmos y Miranda, whichever way he or she prefers. If the preference is just one of the last names, it is usually the first of the two, for example: Julia Olmos.

CHA-CHANGE

To: Moira, Mike, Megan, Josh, Johnny, Sammy
From: Selma
Re: Your bonus is in

Hello Team!

You have bonus checks waiting for you in your mailboxes. You can pick them up anytime.

Thanks,
Selma

PS Acknowledgment appreciated.

They will undoubtedly run and get their bonus checks, but team members should also acknowledge Selma's email.

The reply:

I HEAR YA

To: Selma
From: Moira
Re: Your bonus is in

Thanks for the heads up!

Selma knows at least that Moira got the word.

Email has enough impersonal features of its own without having users introduce more. Remember to add a personal touch to your email messages by using greetings and closings. Would you enter your boss's office and say, "Here is the report. Please let me know if you have any questions. Thanks." Chances are you would probably say hello and your boss's name, and then chat for a few moments. So why be terse or impersonal on email? Life is personal. Remember the "hello/good-bye rule": Always include a form of hello and good-bye in your emails. Otherwise, people might say good-bye to you for good.

How do I abbreviate the word postscript?

The abbreviation for postscript is PS with no punctuation.

CHAPTER 5

SUBJECT HEADERS

#8: DON'T *send emails without subject headers, or with improperly denoted headers.*

With all of the emails that people receive every day, yours should stand out. People will be sure to open emails, for example, with catchy subject headers. Some people will open an intriguing subject before an urgent one (we don't recommend that). But you can be sure that a non-header will be opened last. And you never want to be last on the list.

THE BLANK STARE

To: Robb Watters
From: Sal Vatore
Re: No subject

My partner and I would like to use your services. Could you please call us this afternoon? It is very important.

I am not sure what this email is about. What is the topic? The Re: section gives no indication, nor does the email itself. With emails like this, how am I to determine its urgency when I screen the list of emails in my mailbox?

THE MISMATCH

To: Sally Jefferson
From: Thomas Hemings
Re: Thanksgiving
Date: July 1

Hi!

What time should I come over for the July 4th BBQ?

Thanks,
Tom

You meant to change the subject header to July 4th, right?

THIS EMAIL IS REPEATING ON ME

To: Staff
From: Office Manager
Re: Re: Re: Re: Re: Re: Re: Re: Re: Re: Re: Re:
Re: Re: Re: Re: Re: Re: Re: Re: Re: Re: Re: Re:
Re: Re: Re: Re: Re: Re: Re: Re: Re: Re: Re: Re:
Re: Re: Re: Re: Re: Re: Re: Re: Re: Re: Re: Re:
Re: Re: Re: Re: Re: Re: Re: Re: Re: Re: Re: Re:
Re: Re: Re: Re: Re: Re: Re: Re: Re: Re: Re: Re:
Re: Re: Re: Re: Re: Re: Re: Re: Re: Re: Re: Re:
Re: Re: Re: Re: Interoffice bachelorette party

Hello Staff,

It's already time for Janette's baby shower.

Join us at 3 p.m. in the office lounge for our
toast to Janette!

Thanks,
Office Manager

*This email header has been an ongoing dialogue for one year
about Janette's office bachelorette party and nobody bothered
to change the header, even when Janette was having a baby.
Somebody please change the header. Beware of the runaway
Re:.*

*How do I use punctuation with quotation
marks?*

Periods and commas go inside the quotation
marks. Colons, semicolons, and question
marks go outside.

> **#8: DO** *use subject headers in all of your emails so that the recipient can quickly reference your incoming email and know what it is about.*

E-Guidelines For Subject Headers

Imagine you're starting your day at your desk and you have 57 emails and it's only 8:45 a.m. Which ones do you open first? If you have no idea what they are about, you will probably save the "No Subject" emails for last. We know we do.

Subject headers are used to label emails so that the recipient can know with a quick glance at his or her incoming emails what the email is about. Most people in the business world today not only send and receive emails, but they have to sort through emails based on subject matter. Using a header is also useful for the sender, who generally has backup files of emails that have been sent, and can use the headers to help sort through the messages. Specific subject headers such as "Today's meeting," "The Environment Project," "Personnel issues," and "Happy hour," are much more helpful than "Subject: None" or "Subject: Hi!" (How many of those do we all get?)

Another benefit of using headers is getting noticed. Writing emails to people is one thing, but getting people to open them is another. Always remember that catchy headers are more likely to catch people's attention. Here are a few irresistible headers:

AN OFFER YOU CAN'T REFUSE

From: Russell Rowe
Subject: Tell us more today

Hi,

My partner and I would like to use your services. Could you please call us this afternoon?

It is very important.

Thanks,
Russ

This will get the attention it deserves.

When writing words in a series, separated by commas, is there a need to put a comma after the second to last word in the series (before the "and")?

Including the comma is preferable. Although going without a comma after the second to last item in a series is acceptable, use a comma to avoid confusion. For example: Luther and Jeremy went online to buy a car, stereo speakers, a bed, and a tennis racket.

MUST SEE

From: Anna Stealth
Subject: Urgent meeting

To All Staff,

There will be an important meeting in Zachary's office at 2 p.m. today. Everyone must attend.

This is serious,

Anna

HERE'S THE 411

From: Arnold White
Subject: Important number needed

Hi Folks,

Does anyone have a contact at the Chamber of Commerce?

Thanks in advance,

Arnie

How do I denote italics in my email, for instance, when I refer to the Washington Post*?*

Quotes can double for denoting italicized text. For example: "The Washington Post" is located on 15th Street in Washington, DC.

IS THERE SUCH A THING?

From: Management
To: Junior Staff
Subject: There is a free lunch today

Hi Junior Staff,

We would like to invite all of you out to lunch today. Please respond by 11:30 a.m.

Thanks and see you soon.
Us

What an eye-catcher.

Do I capitalize time zones?

Keep time zones lowercased: eastern daylight time. However, capitalize the abbreviation: EDT. Capitalize only if one of the words is a proper noun: Greenwich mean time.

Bonus: Top Ten Subject Headers
By Chase and Trupp

The following subject headers make our favorites list. Each exhibits the sender's voice and gives the recipient an idea of what the email is about. People will want to open up your email if you write an enticing subject header.

10. What a night!

9. Night skiing

8. Bean counting

7. The answer to your question

6. Cookies in my office

5. Hoping for your input

4. Please read now—code blue!

3. Decisions, decisions

2. Tonight's plans rhyme with "sappy sour"

1. Wondering where you are?

Maybe you have read or written clever subject headers. Please visit us at www.dontstubyourpinkie.com and feel free to share them with us.

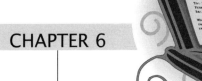

CHAPTER 6

WHEN TO SEND URGENT EMAILS

> **#7: DON'T** *send urgent emails without labeling them as such; and don't assume the receiver has received your email—follow up. Don't label emails as urgent that aren't.*

Would you call 911 and report a fashion mistake? We hope not. So please only mark emails as urgent when they are.

People in today's busy business world don't like to be teased with phoney urgent emails. When you do have an urgent email to send, don't assume that the recipient has received it. Some urgent email blunders:

OUT TO LUNCH IN MORE WAYS THAN ONE

To: Brian Shaw
From: Cracker Staffer
Re: Meeting

Come to the conference room ASAP.

You check your email several times a day, but stepped out at noon for a one-hour lunch. This email was sent at 12:20 p.m.

THE "RESPOND IMMEDIATELY" HOAX

To: Everyone
From: Your Friend
Re: Respond immediately

The first five people who respond to this email will win a trip to the Caribbean!

These email hoaxes are rarely true. Gimmicks are exactly what they sound like.

THE POTENTIAL VIRUS EMAIL

To: Everyone I Know
From: Betty Lang
Re: Open immediately!

Be suspicious of some urgent emails, particularly if you don't know the sender. Some emails addressed with "Urgent, open now" (or a similar emergency come-on) contain viruses, usually within attached files. Delete the files without opening them.

IT REALLY WASN'T URGENT, NOW WAS IT?

To: Bob Alexander
From: Ted Platz
Re: Urgent

Hi Bob,

I am thinking about taking the staff on a company picnic next May.

Your thoughts?

Thanks,

Ted

Was this really urgent? So the next time Ted sends an email you might not open it immediately.

THREATS AND OTHER METHODS

To: All
From: Accounting Staff Manager
Re: Read this!

We will require everyone to have his or her vital information to us by noon today—**or else!**

When did that nice lady in accounting start talking this way? She "sounds" so different on email.

THE EMAIL THAT CAN'T REACH EVERYONE

To: Office
From: Office Manager (a.k.a. the Coffee Nazi)
Re: No brew for you

Beginning today, we will no longer provide coffee to employees.

This is a case of conveying information important to many— at least to the coffee lovers in the office—by a system that doesn't reach everyone. What about the departments, such as accounting, that are not yet linked to the email system? One accounting employee grumbled when the coffee machines vanished without a trace. To play it safe, post the new rules near the coffee machine for those accounting colleagues. Repeat these kinds of messages in other venues: memos, company newsletters, department meetings. Also, the tone of this email leaves a lot to be desired—especially when you consider it is going to people who haven't had their morning coffee yet.

TOO LATE NEWS

To: Buccaneers Work team
From: Team Leader
Re: Meeting
Time: 8:50 a.m.

Hi All,

Our meeting has been rescheduled for 9 a.m. today.

Thanks,
Me

This information would have been more helpful yesterday. Wouldn't there have been a better vehicle, other than email, for this urgent message, such as the telephone?

> **#7: DO** *label urgent emails, and only urgent emails, as such in the subject header; and always follow up with a phone call.*

E-Guidelines For Urgent Emails

Label emails that are time sensitive as "Urgent" in the header. Many people get dozens of emails daily; help them decide which ones are most important. **If the email is not urgent then do not label it as such.** Some email systems, such as Lotus Notes and Microsoft Outlook, allow you to mark an email as high priority, thus telling the system that it should send the email over the firewall as quickly as possible. Because some people don't check their email several times a day, it is advisable to follow up with the recipient via a phone call or personal visit, if possible, to make sure they know an urgent email is headed their way. Don't always assume your receiver has received the email. He or she could be away on business or vacation.

A nice feature that shows the sender when the recipient has received the email is *auto receipt*. Another function of auto receipt is that in some cases it will tell you if the recipient has actually opened the email. These are two different functions. Don't always assume that the recipient has read the email carefully, though. Sometimes we open our emails and simply scan them, or we get distracted by the phone or an office mate and don't finish reading them, or we simply don't have the time to read all of our emails. You wouldn't always assume that your snail-mail letter reached its recipient, would you? You might check on an important letter with a phone call. Or you might send it via registered mail in the first place.

How does the sender determine which emails are urgent? Good question. For the receiver, the subject header (e.g. "Urgent") and name of the sender (e.g. the boss) are telling signs of the importance of the email. For the sender, a good policy is to denote emails as urgent when they require a reply within that same day.

The rule of thumb for replying to urgent emails is to respond as soon as you receive and read the email.

THE SCARY EMAIL

From: Accounting
To: All
Subject: Read now

Hello from Accounting,

We will expect everyone to have vital information to us by noon today. We will also be reminding you in person.

See you soon,
Accounting Department

An urgent email from the people who process your paychecks is one to open.

Is it acceptable to write my emails in smaller than standard font size? I like to get people's attention.

No. Use a minimum of 10-point font size. Anything smaller is a strain on the eyes and unprofessional. See chapter 11 for more details.

ANOTHER SCARY ONE

From: Senior management
To: Everyone
Subject: Urgent 10 a.m. meeting

Hi Everyone,

We are having an urgent staff meeting at 10 a.m. today in the conference room. All are expected to attend.

See you there,
Management

To be on the safe side, don't forget to call people as well. Sometimes people, even diligent email readers, cannot get to their emails first thing in the morning.

COFFEE NAZI SOFTENS UP

To: Office
From: Office Manager
Re: No brew for you

To all concerned,

Beginning today, we will no longer provide coffee to employees. We apologize for any inconvenience this causes.

Stella

This is a much more pleasant way to break bad news.

Don't leave things to chance. Use the appropriate follow-up measures when sending urgent emails. Confirm, confirm, confirm. Too many misunderstandings occur between people who don't know how often others check email. Call people, visit them in person, or even post signs to get people's attention. Have backup plans for urgent situations, especially if you will not be able to reach the recipients by telephone or in person. If you frequently or even occasionally send urgent emails to staff members, you might ask everyone on the list to give you his or her emergency contact.

How do I denote morning and afternoon in emails when referring to time?

Use lowercase a.m. and p.m. It also is acceptable to write it out: I come to work at 9:00 in the morning.

CHAPTER 7

PRIVATE AND CONFIDENTIAL EMAILS

> **#6: DON'T** *send private or confidential information over email.*

Big brother may not be watching you, but he's close by. We've gotten to the point where we're so savvy about the Internet that we may take our emails for granted.

The rule of thumb (or pinkie) in email communication is that nothing is private on email.

UNDER COVER

To: Julia
From: Arnold
Re: The confidential report

Hi Julia,

I have attached the confidential report that I will be presenting at the board meeting next month. I think I have discovered that our company is losing millions of dollars. Will you please read the report? What do you think?

Thanks,
Arnold

I'll tell you what I think. Don't even think about sending confidential materials with email. Too many people have access to your emails.

DISCUSSING OTHER COLLEAGUES

To: Lola
From: Rita
Re: Intern

Our new intern is so hot! Think he'll go out with me?

Can you say... trouble (not to mention sexual harassment)? This message could be forwarded to the wrong person, and you could be involved in a human resources nightmare.

PERSONAL SOLICITATIONS AT WORK

To: My Staff
From: Your Boss
Re: Charity fund-raiser

My husband and I are raising money for the homeless shelter. Please come by my office to donate your funds. Every little bit counts!

Check out the office policy on solicitations at work before sending this email. This is not a work-related charity. I am feeling pressure to give!

L.A. CONFIDENTIAL

To: Ruth
From: Eddie
Re: Confidential

Hi!

This is confidential. I just got a job offer from our client in L.A.!

Me

Do you really think this is confidential? There are backup files in your office that your office manager is monitoring as we speak.

BE CAREFUL WHOM YOU TRUST

To: Jane Lee
From: Roxanne Sommers
Re: The boss

Jane,

I hate our boss. She is a real bitch. Her behavior toward me today was really shitty.

Roxanne

Do you realize your email can be forwarded to the boss with just a click?

To: The Boss
From: Jane Lee
Re: FWD: The boss

Hi Boss,

Thought you would find this information useful.

Thanks,
Jane

Jane has forwarded Roxanne's message verbatim to the boss. Be cautious about what you write and about whom you write because you never know where your email will land.

> **#6: DO** *remember that no email is sacred. Be careful when sending private or confidential information in emails.*

E-Guidelines For Private Or Confidential Emails

Rule of thumb for emails: When writing an email just think of the "Everyone Rule." This rule assumes everyone and anyone you know (or don't know) could possibly see your email. Netiquette experts, who create guidelines for email and Internet use, suggest that people think before they send email. Would you want your children, priest or rabbi, grandmother, or boss to read this email? Or the government? Is it suitable, appropriate, or even *legal*? According to one Netiquette expert, "if your email is not suitable for a postcard, don't send it at all." (See www.marketing.tenagra.com/rfc1855.) Your emails are the equivalent of postcards. Think about how many hands a postcard crosses before it gets to the recipient—and then apply that analogy to your last email. By policing yourself, you are careful about what you write. So, don't disparage your boss on email! And, keep in mind that no love letter or nefarious scheme is sacred.

Remember that confidentiality cannot be assured in emails. Your system administrator has access to your files, for example, through backup files. An unlimited number of people have access to your email, from office administrators to hackers, so please be careful when including personal tidbits or confidential reports in your emails.

If you are uncomfortable when someone emails you personal information or questionable information (such as a risqué joke), ask this person kindly not to write anything personal in nature over email anymore, or at least not to your business email address. You can discuss personal details through your home email address, over the phone, or, if your recipient is local, over drinks. Each office has its own guidelines on the use of company email for personal communication. Find out what the rules are. Even if it is okay for you to use your company email for personal reasons, keep in mind the "Everyone Rule."

In many businesses, such as law firms, credit card companies, consulting firms, doctors' offices, accounting firms, and banks, privacy and confidentiality are crucial for success. Mistakes can cost you your job. Ask your office manager about office policies for transmitting confidential business information via email.

TIP: If you would like to send a confidential message to someone, skip the details and provide information only people "in the know" can understand. Think of it as a code. Or you can send an email requesting a telephone or in-person conversation, so that you can have a private discussion.

GETTING PERSONAL

To: Victor
From: Joel
Re: Personnel—important

Hi Victor,

Can we get together to discuss a personnel issue? It is important that I speak with you in person.

Thanks,
Joel

Understood. When Joel sends an email saying that he wants to discuss "personnel" issues, Victor knows to get in touch with Joel to set up a meeting. The last time they met about such issues, Joel told Victor that there would soon be layoffs company wide—important intelligence. It is best to discuss such sensitive issues in person.

> *In which cases would I use "among" and "between?"*
>
> Use "among" when referring to a group of more than two. Use "between" when referring to a group of two. For example: The seven children shared the apples among themselves. Jesse and Lawrence shared the chocolate bar between each other.

NO PRESSURE SOLICITATIONS

To: My Staff
From: Victoria
Re: Charity fund-raiser

Hi Everyone,

My husband and I are volunteering to raise money for the homeless shelter. Please come by my office if you would like to donate even the smallest contribution to this important cause.

Thank you,
Vickie

We believe that offices should be off the charity email list. If it is appropriate, however, this would be the way to go.

L.A. CONFIDENTIAL TAKE TWO

To: Patti
From: Kathleen
Re: Good news

Hi Kathleen,

Looks like our friend will be taking a trip to the West after all.

Sending good news,
Patti

Background: During lunch, Patti and Kathleen met at the Elizabeth Arden salon for nail appointments. They discussed the possibility of their friend and colleague, ML, transferring to the L.A. office. ML has had her eye on this transfer for at least a year. Later that afternoon, Patti bumped into ML and discovered that the transfer came through. ML asked Patti to keep it confidential, and to tell only Kathleen. The president will not be announcing the transfer for at least a month. Patti was so ecstatic, she emailed Kathleen just enough information to let her know the good news.

If only we could have some peace and privacy, what a wonderful world it would be. We hope that this chapter has showed you that nothing is sacred; no emails are safe. Use your common sense about sending emails that include confidential or private matters. You will be glad that you did.

CHAPTER 8

SPAMMING

> **#5: DON'T** *spam. Just don't do it, and don't reply to spammers.*

While it may be interesting to take a look at other names on list emails that you receive (we admit it), it really is bad form to use these names for other purposes. It can create chaos and bad feelings, and it will give a negative impression.

THE GENERAL UNSOLICITED EMAIL

To: Shara Jones
From: Your Friend
Re: $$$ Make Money $$$

Dear Shara,

It's me! I wanted you to know about a project we are running that pays $25 per hour. All you have to do is make a few phone calls.

Are you in?

Thanks,
Your Friend at 555-1234.

Who sent me this? I guess they got my email address from someone. Or maybe I gave some random person my business card with my email address. Gotta be careful!

SPAMMING COWORKERS

To: Office Staff
From: Office Manager
Re: Monthly meetings

Hi gang!

I am writing to tell you that our monthly meetings will be moved from the first Monday of the month to the first Tuesday.

Thanks,
Office Manager

Minutes later...

To: Office Staff
From: Richard Kane
Re: Re: Monthly meetings

Hi gang!

Come to Casino Night!

Lots o' fun prizes!

For Charity!

Where: Hilton

When: 8 p.m. Friday

Bring a partner with you. Just $350 per person! Remember it's for charity! Don't forget to drop off your canned goods at the door and you will get a free drink upon entry!

Thanks,
Richard

Why would I want this email? Shouldn't this person check with office policy before using someone else's email list as his own? See chapter 3, Mass Emails. The same guidelines for the use of mailing lists applies here.

HOLIDAY BLUES

To: Everyone in the Office
From: Your Friendly Travel Agent
Re: Vacation—$$$$—Cheap

We can send you to Florida round trip for $19.00 Please call us at 781-XXX-XXX for more details.

This is another one we don't want at the office. Some offices do not allow employees to receive such emails.

TOO HOT TO HANDLE

To: You
From: Your Friend
Re: Hot, hot, hot! XXX: the email you requested

Click on this address: doit.net and you will fulfill your wildest fantasies.

I didn't request this! Who got my address? I don't want this stuff at the office.

HEALTH ALERT

To: Women in the Office
From: Karen Ehrlich
Re: Women, you must read this to save your life

My friend sent this to me today and I want to share it with all of you.

Attention Women:

Women across America are getting the Grumbles. This is a disease that manifests itself in uncontrollable grumbles. It happens in offices, and may be linked to the fluorescent lighting. Here is the latest study...

Send this to ten people today, and you won't get sick. If you don't, you might get the Grumbles yourself.

We absolutely believe in wellness, but this is making us sick!

What are the symbols for "slash" and "backslash?"

A slash is (/) and the backslash is (\). The slash is used frequently in Internet addresses. The backslash is used in some computer operating systems to mark the division between a directory and a subdirectory.

PARTY CIRCUIT USA

To: All Party People in the House
From: Ricky Rox
Re: New Year's Party

The latest and greatest lineup is out for New Year's Eve:

DC—party at the Capitol—black tie
NYC—Trump Tower
Chicago—Chicago Hilton and Towers
LA—Beverly Wilshire

Etc., etc.

I live in Tulsa. Why am I getting this email?

SPORTS TICKETS OFFERINGS

To: Joe Johnson
From: Tourney Man
Re: Tennis tournament

We have 100 tickets for the grand tennis open here in Springfield. The first 100 people to respond to this email can buy the courtside tickets.

How do these people get my name?

> **#5: DO** *be considerate when sending unsolicited emails.*

E-Guidelines For Spamming

A lot of that rubbish you receive in your traditional mailbox is being replaced by the rubbish in your virtual mailbox. When someone sends you junk email, contact your email provider for assistance.

Sending

Spamming is when a person sends unsolicited emails to others. (Don't be embarrassed if you thought a spam had to do with a canned meat item. Many of us did at first.) The spammers can get your email address in a number of ways. The primary way for spammers to get your email address is through buying "email lists" from companies that compile such lists. Other ways to get spammed are by distributing your business email indiscriminately or by being part of a long forwarding list that was used for other purposes. Don't send an unsolicited email unless you are fairly sure the recipient would want to receive it. On the other hand, if you are a businessperson and buy an email list, keep in mind the rules of spamming. It can be acceptable to send unsolicited email if it's done properly, as we said in chapter 3. Consult an expert in email solicitations. To learn online how to send a polite unsolicited business email, you can refer to www.copywriter.com/lists/.

The Reply All Feature

Many emailers are guilty of spamming a list that someone else sends them. Be considerate of forwarded email lists. If you receive a forwarded email, and the list of receivers is included on the email, please do not use this list for yourself. If you are the original sender, use the BCC function so your list can't be misused, especially when you have the addresses of confidential clients on the list.

Receiving

When receiving an unsolicited message, do not respond. Tell your system administrator, your office manager, or contact your email provider to see if they have guidelines on how to handle a spammer. Sometimes spammers will include in their messages a reply address you can contact to take you off of their list. Or, in some cases, the spammer will block your reply, and you will not be able to send an email to that address. What your system administrator might suggest is writing to postmaster@thatparticulardomain.com to file a complaint with the administrator there. There are also plenty of anti-spam Web sites to consult, such as bigfoot.com for more advice.

What is the plural of 1900?

The plural of years is denoted by adding an "s" only. So the plural of 1900 is 1900s—not 1900's with an apostrophe (a common mistake). For example: In the late 1900s, the Internet became popular.

Go Gators

An email goes around the office offering free tickets to the Gators game from an outside organization. You are on that list. What do you do?

LATER GATOR

> **To:** postmaster@thatemailaddress.com
> **From:** Josephine
> **Re:** Gators tickets
>
> Hello,
>
> I received the Gators tickets email. Would you please remove my name from your group email list?
>
> Thank you,
> Josephine

Contact your system administrator for advice about this. This reply would work best for a sender that you do not know and doesn't *have a blocked email address. If your reply to the spammer is blocked, delete any other correspondence from this source. Consult with your system administrator or software company about how they recommend you deal with the spammer.*

LATER TO ALL THE GATORS

To: Jeffrey, Sam, Reggie, Al, Hunter, etc.
From: Josephine
Re: Gators tickets

Hi All,

My name is Josephine and I received an email from Jessica about Gators tickets. Please delete my name from your list. This email is a private address. Thanks. I appreciate it.

Best regards,
Josephine

This method works best if you know the senders.

GREAT LIST; CAN I USE IT?

Here is what you can do if you would like to use the list: Get the permission of the sender and all those who are on the list.

To: Jessica
From: Josephine
Re: Gators tickets

Hi Jessica,

Thanks for the email you sent me and some of your other friends about the tickets to the Gators game. Would it be all right if I emailed some people on your list to see if they would like to attend the Citrus Bowl?

Thanks,
Josephine

This is a good first step, but you should then ask permission of those on the entire list. If you get a positive response, go for it.

THERE'S NO BUSINESS LIKE EMAIL BUSINESS

To: Your Name
From: joseph@worldsbestprinter.com
Re: Office services, fair fees

Hello,

My name is Joseph and I opened the World's Best Printer shop right here in Downtown. I would like to invite you to come to our store at 6301 South Westshore Drive. We offer the best prices in the area for printing services. Please consider us in the future when you have printing needs. Thank you for your time.

Example of fees: 100 copies (black and white) for $3.00. That's three cents per copy.

Best wishes,
Joseph at World's Best Printers

PS To remove yourself from this list, please email postmaster@worldsbestprinter.com.

Joseph bought an email list and sent this mass solicitation email. He was concise and polite. It can be done, but very delicately. Proceed with caution.

Oh, what is this world coming to? Last year I had to worry about cell phones scrambling my brain, and now it's this spamming business. Well, rest assured you are not alone. You have friends to turn to, such as your system administrator and your software company, for advice. Find out their recommendations for the proper steps in dealing with spammers.

CHAPTER 9

RESPONDING TO EMAILS

#4: DON'T *ignore incoming emails by not responding (unless they're spam).*

The big debate is over whether or not you have to respond to each email you receive and, what the acceptable time frame is for sending a response. Yes, please respond to urgent emails as soon as possible. Respond by the end of the day to emails that require an answer, but no deadline is given. We will repeat this message in our e-guide-lines because it is so important.

It's simply bad business to ignore people. Every client and colleague should be treated with dignity.

PLEASE ANSWER

To: Deborah Hubbard, Judy Mohler, Gail Nicely
From: Debbie Alden
Re: Urgent

Who can attend this month's meeting in San Francisco?

Need to know by COB Friday.

[No response]

This was an urgent email. Where is everybody? They are on Debbie's team, they're in the office, and they use email daily—yet they don't respond. (COB, by the way, doesn't have anything to do with corn. It is a commonly used email acronym for close of business. See the glossary for more email terms.)

Is there a difference between "disinterested" and "uninterested?"

Yes. Disinterested means "non-biased." Uninterested means not interested at all.

FORGOT TO TELL PEOPLE I'M ON VACATION

To: Lois
From: Claire
Re: Urgent

I have sent you numerous emails regarding our marketing plan. Please respond before 5:30 p.m. today, or I will take you off the marketing team email list.

Did you remember to tell people you were on vacation? Uh oh.

EARTH TO YOU

To: Harvey
From: Margie
Re: Earth to you

Are you still breathing?

Why do you give out your email to people if you do not intend to check it?

THANK YOU, THANK YOU

To: Kristy Roberts
From: John Rowe
Subject: The gift certificate

Kristy,

Thank you for the gift certificate to Dillard's. I was touched by the gesture, and by the kind words you wrote in the accompanying note. After 10 years of working in our office, I still enjoy going to work every day. Thank you for remembering my anniversary. You are the finest person I have ever worked with, and I look forward to many more happy years here at the office.

Warmest regards,
John

[No response]

The emailed thank you note paid Kristy quite a compliment. Shouldn't she write back?

> **#4: DO** *reply to emails that solicit a response, or even emails you think should be acknowledged.*

E-Guidelines For Email Replies

If you receive an email that warrants a response, you should reply, in most cases, by the end of the day. If you are in an office setting, and want to know how often it is expected of you to check email, speak with the boss or office manager. Or, collectively, your team or entire office could set some email standards—for example, you could agree to check email at least twice per day. If you are the boss and it is up to you to set the rules, the standard is to check at least once per day.

If you only check email once per week, then let people know that when distributing your email address. People who check their email messages often may mistakenly assume that others do likewise. If it has been a week since you checked email, for example, and you come across an email that day that was sent five days earlier, respond right away. Let that person know in your reply that you just received the email, and take this opportunity to tell him or her how often you are checking in. You might miss out, though, on some great, time-sensitive opportunities if you operate on the weekly plan. Don't let that happen. Keep up with the pace: Check at least once per day. Remember, too, not to give your email out to every cyber Tom, Dick, and Harry. Your email address is as sacred as your telephone number and address. Be careful who you let into your life, even in the business world.

Email is like voice mail. You can't be too sure that the person you are trying to reach has received your message, unless you get that person "live." As a *sender*, it is important to be thorough and follow up on your "hanging messages" or unanswered ones. Don't leave anything to chance!

In most cases, though, the obligation in the "reply" situation is not on the sender, but on the recipient. People in the business world today make themselves available 24-7, through email, office telephones, cellular phones, pagers, and other modes of communication. To keep up, you need to be attentive to your various messaging systems, not the least of which is email. People will expect that of you if you are doing business with them.

Mechanics

When replying to an email, you can either construct a new email entirely (find "Compose" or "Write Mail" or the equivalent on your system) or respond to your sender's email by clicking on the "reply" feature included in each email message. By using this method, you will send your response right back to the address from which it came.

Original Message

What information should be included in your reply? When you click on reply, many programs automatically set up your reply to include the entire original message. If that is the case, delete the sender's message. You should include just enough information in your response to let the recipient know to what it is you are replying. Is it easier to include the sender's entire original email in your reply? Sure it is. Click reply. The original email sets the scene. You answer the question. Send email. Case closed.

It may be easier, but this is not the way to go. Why not?

Including both the original email and your response in the reply is simply too much information. Keep it simple. Compare this to a similar situation with voice mail. If someone asks you a question through a voice-mail message, when you call that person back or speak with him or her later, would you repeat word for word the original request and then give your answer? No. You would summarize the thought and set up the context of the question within the frame of your answer.

For example, the boss leaves you a voice mail that begins with a minute-long dialogue about last week's vacation in England, and then she proceeds to ask you to run a report on the February expenses for Client X. When you later catch up with the boss, would you repeat to her all of the information she told you about the Tower of London and Buckingham Palace, and then answer the question? No. She doesn't need to hear that, she knows it already. You would simply answer her request, by noting that you received her voice mail about the report for Client X and then giving the status of the report. You may acknowledge her trip, of course, but repeating it play by play isn't necessary.

Similarly, your original email sender, to whom you are replying, does not want to sort through his or her entire email before getting to your response. He or she wants an *answer*. Please remember to delete the original message, especially with lengthy original emails. Don't tie up your email system, or others, with more information than is needed. Your goal is to simply create a frame of reference for your original sender in the reply. We have some suggestions on how to do that.

Establishing a Frame of Reference

Subject headers are the easiest way of creating a frame of reference for a reply, and sometimes they're all you need.

Subject: The 4 p.m. meeting—are you coming?

The original sender will see this subject header and know immediately what the reply is all about.

If a few words in the header will not suffice clearly to explain the subject, then you can key in a few words or sentences about the topic in the body of your reply email as a reference. If you want to send a really snazzy reply, copy your reference verbatim from the original email into your reply. To do this, highlight the text you would like copied in the original email, then click on reply. Your replied email will begin with the copied portion of the email and will look something like this:

"In a message dated 6/12/01 10:19:06 AM Eastern Daylight Time, originalsender'sname@domain.com writes:

<< When can you get me Robert on the telephone? >>"

And here is where you would begin your reply...

Most email programs are automatically set up to carry out this feature for you. The recipient will know exactly to what you are referring, because you copied the request as a reminder. If your response to the above request is "2 p.m." and you didn't reference the original question in your reply, your original sender might not understand what "2 p.m." by itself means.

This may sound a little tedious, but if you send out 50 emails per day, and several of them are to the same people with similar requests, you might be perplexed when you receive a reply from one that says:

Subject: Request
Hi,
Will do.

Ben

"Will do?" To which request is this person referring? A simple way of creating a frame of reference is just incorporating a small mention into your text. Instead of "will do," you can write something like this:

Hi Ted,
I will hire security for next week's event.

Thanks,

Ben

Auto Signature

The auto signature is also a nice mechanism for letting people know details about you, your title, address, phone number, and even a message or a favorite quote. Many email systems have this feature which appends your signature information to the close of each email you send. It is almost like creating a letterhead for your emails.

TIP: To set up an auto signature, find the option on your tool bar, or under "Tools," or under "Special Features," or use the help option to search for auto signatures. Once you find it, the feature will prompt you to enter the information you would like to be included in the signature. Most programs allow you to set up various signatures.

You may want to use different signatures for different audiences, such as clients, colleagues, or situations.

Remember how we discussed making your emails interesting? This is one of those opportunities.

Kim's Standard Auto Signature

Dear Christopher,

Thanks for the update.

Cheers,
Kim

Kimberly Reese
National Coordinator
The Issues Company
15 Sky Drive
Pine Valley, PA 06543
Telephone: 215-555-1234
Fax: 215-555-1233

Attention recipient: I check my email twice per week. If you need immediate attention, please call me. Thank you and have a wonderful day.

All of the above information is included now automatically in each email that she sends.

Kim's Other Auto Signatures
For staff and colleagues:

Kimberly Reese
Program Coordinator
Telephone: x1234
Fax: 555-1233

A quote of the day for you:
"If you see an elephant stepping on the tail of
a mouse, and you do nothing to help the
mouse, you are taking the side of the aggres-
sor." —Bishop Desmond Tutu

*For emails sent internally on Fridays to colleagues
with whom Kim is also friends:*

Kimberly Reese
Program Coordinator
Telephone: x1234
Fax: 555-1233

TGIF—Have a great weekend!

When using your various auto signatures, remember each
time you set up an email to choose the appropriate auto signature for your recipient. You might not want to send one
of your more casual signatures to your client.

Out-of-Office Reply Tool

A nice feature of more advanced email programs is the "out-
of-office-reply" tool. When you know ahead of time that
you will be out of the office, even for a day, use the out-of-
office reply feature. Find this feature on your tool bar or
listed among the options. Similar to setting up the auto signature, the out-of-office reply tool prompts you to fill in a

message that you would like to send to anyone who emails you while you are out. Keep it short and sweet, and remember to include your departure and arrival dates and an emergency contact and phone number. Once set up, when someone emails you, this feature will automatically kick in and send your pre-created message. Here is a good example of an out-of-office reply:

> Hi,
>
> Thanks for your email. I will be out of the office from Monday the 7th until Tuesday the 8th. Please call my colleague, Ruth, for immediate attention at 675-0933. Otherwise, I will respond to you upon my return to the office on Wednesday, the 9th.
>
> Thanks,
> Ted

Acknowledgment Email

For emails that don't solicit an answer to a question, use the "acknowledgment email." Saying "thanks, I got your email" is a nice way to let people know that you care about what they sent.

LET'S DO LUNCH

The question...

To: Gwen
From: Alison
Re: Lunch

Hi Gwen,

Wow, what a weekend! My husband left for a business trip, and my two sons are sick. I spent yesterday nursing them back to health with lots of liquids and TLC.

How are you? I was thinking about you this weekend and thought it had been some time since we had lunch. Would you like to join me for lunch next Tuesday? You can email me a reply, here, at alison@eee.net

Thanks,
Alison

The reply...

To: Alison
From: Gwen
Re: Re: Lunch

Hi Alison,

Sure, I would love to join you. Let's meet on Tuesday at noon downstairs, and we can go from there. I would love to hear more about how your family is doing.

Thanks,
Gwen

It is perfectly acceptable to reply by email, and best to reply within a day, second best within two days—considering the lunch is a week away, and this email isn't urgent. Gwen's reply has enough information in it to give Alison a good frame of reference. Note the reply does not include the text of the entire original message.

HEY, THANK YOU

To: Richard
From: Emily
Re: Three-year anniversary pen

Richard,

Thanks for the anniversary pen. I will look forward to using it here at work. It is also a reminder of how much I am valued here in the company.

Thanks again,
Emily

The reply...

Emily,

You are welcome! We have had three wonderful years with you. We hope to have many more.

Best,
Richard

Please acknowledge thank you emails. It is a nice touch, and the sender of the original email will know that the thank you note was received. There is no need to continue the flatteries from here. Everyone is squared.

SOUND THE ALARM

The Urgent Email

To: Marcy
From: Hans
Re: URGENT! COMPUTERS DOWN AT 4 P.M. TODAY

Hi Marcy,

Please tell your staff that the computers will be down at 4 p.m. today for testing.

Thanks,
Hans

Ready, set, go! The response...

To: Hans
From: Marcy
Re: Re: URGENT! COMPUTERS DOWN AT 4 P.M. TODAY

Hans,

I will let everyone know immediately.

Thank you,
Marcy

Let Hans know that you are taking care of business. He needs to hear from you.

SOUND THE ALARM, PART II

To: My Staff
From: Marcy
CC: Hans
Re: COMPUTERS DOWN AT 4 P.M. TODAY

Hello Everyone,

The computers will go down at 4 p.m. today for testing. Please be sure to log off before 4 p.m. The computers will be back up in the morning.

Please email me if you have any questions.

Thanks,
Marcy

You can also let Hans know you have received the message by copying him on your letter to your staff. If time is of the essence, this is a good way to communicate with Hans and your staff at once.

How often should I check my email throughout the day?

How heavily does your business rely on email communication? If not much, then check twice per day. If moderately (some clients and colleagues email you), then check between three to five times daily. If you are in a type of work that relies almost exclusively on email communication, check frequently, about 10 times per day.

ANOTHER NERVE-RACKING DEADLINE

Assignment Due–Needs Response

To: Gardenia@theseflowersaresobeautiful.com
From: Rosie@willthisdayeverend.com
Re: Assignment due

Hi Gardenia,

The client just called and requested that you work up a report on the latest event expenses by 5 p.m. Friday. Please let me know if this works with your schedule.

Thanks,
Rosie

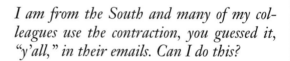

I am from the South and many of my colleagues use the contraction, you guessed it, "y'all," in their emails. Can I do this?

If the email is informal, and y'all is a frequently used term between you and the recipient, then you can use it. If you do not know the recipient, you can be the judge of its usage. For more formal email correspondence, you might want to stick with the more conventional "all of you."

And your reply...

To: Rosie@willthisdayeverend.com
From:
Gardenia@theseflowersaresobeautiful.com
Re: Re: Assignment due

"In a message dated 12/19/00 7:15:02 AM
Eastern Standard Time,
rosie@willthisdayeverend.com writes:

<< The client just called and requested that
you work up a report on the latest event
expenses by 5 p.m. Friday. Please let me know
if this works with your schedule? >>"

Hi, Rosie:

I would be happy to have that assignment for
you on Friday. I will run it by you on Friday
morning, and then have the final version
ready by COB Friday.

Thanks,
Gardenia

*Rosie gives assignments to Gardenia almost every day. From
the subject header, it is unclear as to which assignment is due.
Gardenia used a portion of the text from the original message to clarify the assignment. What an aromatic exchange.*

SORRY, GOTTA RUN

To: Ann
From: Joseph
Re: Rankings

Hi Ann,

Do you have the latest rankings on graduate schools? I am interviewing a student from a Virginia school, and I would like to know where the school's program ranks.

Thanks,
Joseph

The reply...

Dear Joseph,

Your question: "Do you have the latest rankings on graduate schools?"

The answer: The annual report comes out in three months. I can bring you last year's report. I don't think the rankings change drastically from year to year. I'll drop it off in a few minutes.

Thanks,
Ann

Ann keyed in part of Joseph's original message as a reference. It works.

CHECK IN, BUT YOU DON'T CHECK OUT

To: Rachel
From: Jagruti
Re: New club for women
Rachel,

I was thinking of getting a group of women together to start a salon. Would you like to organize it with me?

Thanks,
Jagruti

Response three weeks later...

Hi Jagruti,

It was great to get your email. I don't check my emails often. I would be delighted to help organize a salon. Please feel free to send me all of the details.

Thanks,
Rachel

This is a perfectly acceptable response. Your recipient knows that you don't check your email address frequently. That is okay—it is not expected of you.

LEAVIN' ON A JET PLANE

Auto Reply–Out of Office

To: John
From: Sydney
Re: Tennis

Hey John,

Would you like to get together at the executive club upstairs for a game of tennis tomorrow?

Thanks,
Sydney

Response...

To: Sydney
From: John
Re: Auto Reply: Out of Office, Re: Tennis

Hello,

I will be out of the office from today, Wednesday, through Friday. I will be back in the office on Monday.

Looking forward to getting back to you on Monday.

Thanks,
John

Replies are wonderful if they are concise yet informative. Remember to include just enough information about the original email to set up a context in your reply, but nothing more. We are big believers in efficiency and brevity.

CHAPTER 10

SPELLING AND GRAMMAR DO MATTER

#3: DON'T *use poor spelling and/or grammar in emails.*

Just taking the time to read through and check your spelling can mean so much to your clients and colleagues. It could mean the difference in a promotion or getting new business. Poor spelling and typos are a turnoff, like chatting with someone who has something caught in their teeth. It leaves an uncomfortable feeling. So pause in all the rushing around and take the time (usually only a few moments) to read and spell check your finished emails.

Many users are not aware that their email program probably has a built-in spell check feature. To locate this feature, look under "Tools" or "Special Features" or try "Help." Do not, however, let the spell checker be your last line of defense. Get into the habit of spell checking your emails and *then* reading them one last time. The spell checker will catch

When do you use "that" and when do you use "which"?

"That" introduces a restrictive clause (essential to the sentence), and "which" introduces a nonrestrictive clause (a descriptive clause that would not change the significance of the sentence if omitted). "Which" is almost always preceded by a comma and "that" generally is not.

For example: The computer that the president purchased cost $3,000. (This offers essential information, because it describes a specific computer.)

The computer, which cost $3,000, was stolen from the office. (The cost of the computer is not essential information in this sentence.)

obvious misspellings such as "hte" for "the," but it can't read your mind. Do you mean "you" or "your"? Both of them look okay to the spell checker.

SPELL CHECK-PLEASE!

To: The Staff
From: Management
Re: Spelling and grammer

Please make certain that you chek the speling when you send out proposels and emails to the the client.

Can someone help this person find the spell checker?

WHAT LANGUAGE IS THIS?

To: Syble Earnest
From: Sis Salawich
Re: Outtey

Outta here! Leavin' 2day @ 4 cos I need some zzzzzz's.

C Ya!

I'm not sure I follow. Proper English is easier to read.

PUNCTUATION

To: Rachel Anistonis, Scott Major, Diedre Foster
From: Joe Figgs
Re: Timmy Hennigan

Hi all

When are we leaving for the luncheon

Can Robb drive us there

Thanks
JF

Shouldn't there be a couple of question marks and other punctuation here?

SPELLING-REVISITED

To: Staff
From: Management
Re: Party

We are having our annual Chrismas and Kanucka party this Friday.

All are welcome.

Think about how many people are reading this and wondering what a Kanucka is and where the "t" in Christmas went. And this is from your managers, the people who are supposed to be leading you. This is like receiving a note from your child's English teacher riddled with typos and incorrect grammar.

> **#3: DO** *remember to check your spelling and grammar.*

E-Guidelines

Write the contents of your email the way you would in a letter, adhering to the rules of English grammar. Many email programs have a built-in spell check mechanism. Too many people stub their pinkie on the space bar by using bad

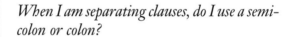

When I am separating clauses, do I use a semicolon or colon?

Generally speaking, the semicolon (;) is used to separate two clauses that are complete thoughts themselves but are closely related and have been written to form a compound sentence. For example: The Internet is growing more powerful by the day; it has virtually replaced snail mail communication.

The colon (:) is typically used to separate two independent clauses in which the second clause explains or amplifies the first. If a sentence can stand by itself after a colon, the first word after the colon is capitalized. For example: The employees were on strike: This was a direct result of the company-wide salary freeze.

spelling, poor grammar, and a host of other language no-no's. Most of us would not allow ourselves to make these mistakes in other written forms of communication. Remember, email is not a license to use bad spelling. Use spell check. If your system does not have it, then proofread your writing carefully, just like people did in the '80s.

I BEFORE E

To: Gerald Levey
From: Judy Gideon
Re: Event tonight

Hi Gerry,

We are scheduled to receive our guests at 7 p.m. tonight in the hotel's Excalibur Room, on the second floor. I look forward to seeing you then.

Thank you,
Judy

Before I ran the spell check program on this email, I had two misspellings: "recieve" and "hte," the latter being my most common email mistake.

The verdict is in: if your emails have typos, spelling mistakes, and grammar problems, you are not portraying yourself in a professional light. Take the extra time to make a good impression.

?

I am terrified of hyphens. When should I use them?

The trend is to drop hyphens, unless the meaning of the word is unclear.

"Pro," "non," and "anti" are generally used without hyphens: prolife, nonpartisan, anti-war protestors, etc., unless the word is vague: anti-female. However, "self-" and "quasi-" are still hyphenated. When using compound words as an adjective, use a hyphen to avoid ambiguity. For example: best-selling author, slow-cooked ribs.

If the meaning of the compound words seem unclear to you, use *The Chicago Manual of Style*'s fast-sailing ship rule. Use of a hyphen depends upon the meaning of the sentence. For example: A fast-sailing ship is a ship that sails fast, but a fast sailing ship is a sailing ship that moves fast.

Don't be afraid—or too busy—to use a dictionary. This handy reference tool spells out the answers to all of your hyphenation questions.

CHAPTER 11

USING CAPITAL AND LOWERCASE LETTERS

#2: DON'T *use all CAPITAL or all lowercase letters in email, and don't use an extremely small font so that people can hardly read what you are writing.*

So many people have told us that they really hate being yelled at via email. Using all caps in your emails expresses either anger or joy—or a complete lack of respect and concern for your reader. A message written in all caps is much more difficult to read than one written using proper capitalization. Marketing professionals know to save the all caps for short, attention-grabbing headlines. A good rule of thumb: Do not use more than three words in caps.

Emails also suffer from the opposite problem: the use of mouse type and all lowercase that comes across as someone who speaks so low and quietly that it's impossible to hear him or her.

We have media-trained many people in the art of projecting their voices during presentations and media interviews. It's important to impart your message clearly, and to make it easy for your audience to understand what you're saying. The same advice applies to email messages. All lowercase messages—as well as all cap messages—are more difficult to decipher and leave a less than positive impression with your audience. We've said it once but it

---

When do I use exclamation marks? People use them all the time in email.

Use the exclamation mark sparingly—for a bold statement and commands. For example: Do not write "I am so tired!" Instead write, "I have never been more exhausted in my life!" And if you do have to use an exclamation mark, never use more than one.

bears repeating: Email is not a license to chuck the rules of proper language usage, including capitalization rules.

TURN DOWN THE VOLUME

To: Entire Global Office
From: Jenny Savage
Re: WHAT ARE YOU THINKING?

WHO LEFT THE BATHROOM WITHOUT CHANGING THE TOILET PAPER ROLL? I WENT TO THE BATHROOM AND THERE WAS NO PAPER IN THE STALL! YOUR MOTHER DOES NOT LIVE HERE! CHANGE IT YOURSELF!

I feel as if I'm being yelled at. And I don't even use the restroom in the Miami office from which this email originated. I'm in L.A. All caps indicate you are shouting.

WHAT? I CAN'T HEAR YOU!

To: global office
From: the director
Re: promotion

we are pleased to announce that jennifer has worked so hard as an assistant sales rep that she is now a full-fledged sales rep! congrats, jennie!

Does this give Jennie the credit she deserves?

FONT

To: Robert W. Farnsworth IX
From: Jonathon Joseph
Re: Thanks

Dear Trustee,

We are pleased to tell you that your dollars are making a big impact on campus. Thank you for your thoughtful contribution.

Sincerely,
The President of Your University

Is this looking a bit casual for a thank you letter to the $30 million donor? Maybe you can find an even funkier font to turn off your cash cow!

COLOR

To: All Staff
From: The Manager
Re: Accounting policy

[Note: because we cannot show red type in a black and white book, imagine the text in the following message as all red.]

Dear Staff:

There will be a session on accounting in the conference room tomorrow. We want to keep things in the black.

Sincerely,
Office Management

Color can sometimes have meanings on many different levels. When we imagine this email being sent in red, we are thinking: "in the red," which isn't good. Before you send a red email to your accounting team, or a purple and yellow email to your boss, consider basic black. Perhaps you can save the red, white, and blue email for the office Independence Day party.

THE MICRO-MINI

To: Sam
From: Harry
Re: Memo

Charles, can you please get that memorandum to me by 5 p.m.?

Thanks,

Kenneth

Mouse type is not an attention-getter. My eyes are exhausted after reading this 6-point type. It's annoying. I need a magnifying glass to read it.

How can I communicate a word or phrase that stands out in my email, without using all capital letters?

Type an asterisk before and after the word or words you would like to be bolded, or that you would like to stand out. For example: Email is the *only* form of communication to use with our client. He uses a pseudonym and does not wish for his identity to be known.

> **#2: DO** *reserve caps for when you want to convey a loud or shouting message. Use all lowercase if you are conveying a whisper in your email. Use at least a 10-point font size.*

E-Guidelines For Capital And Lowercase Letters

1. WHAT IS YOUR IMPRESSION OF THIS SENTENCE?

2. and this one?

3. How about this one?

The first sentence uses all capital letters and has the effect of shouting at the reader. Plus it is difficult to read. Our advice? Stay away from all capital letters (all caps).

Sentence #2 does not start with a capital letter. When in business, remember to adhere to the rules of grammar, such as using a capital letter at the beginning of a sentence. These rules have a purpose, such as indicating to the reader where a sentence begins and ends. Also, this micro-mini sentence practically requires a magnifying glass to read—the type is so small. Do not venture smaller than a 10-point font if you want your readers to be able to read the email.

Finally, look at sentence #3: a capital letter at the beginning of the sentence, lowercase letters for all words other than proper nouns, and a standard 12-point font. Looks good.

Also, be careful with the use of color in emails. Use color when you think the occasion is appropriate. Think black for more serious and standard emails. For more fun or casual correspondence, color can be used, such as for a thank you note or an office party invitation.

IT GOT MY ATTENTION

To: Entire Office
From: Abby
Re: Staff Notice: Bathroom

Hello everyone,

Effective immediately, please clean up after yourself in the bathroom. Our janitor will not start until next week, so we have to be mindful of each other, and clean up after each use. That means that you must throw away all paper towels you use, and replenish toilet paper. The toilet paper can be found in the cabinet inside each bathroom.

If you have any questions or concerns, please see me. I will revisit the situation again in one week.

Thank you for your cooperation and patience,
Abby

You've really cleaned up your act. Thank you!

WHEN CAPS ARE OKAY

To: Vernon
From: Grant
Re: Great news

Hello Vernon,

Great news! Our bid was accepted. We now have a new client, Washington Industries, and the contract was approved for $14 million!

I wanted to let you know right away. Let's celebrate.

WAY TO GO!

From,
Grant

The writer of this email shows his enthusiasm with exclamation marks, and uses all caps for his brief finale. He really is shouting, with joy!

It is possible to relay feelings, such as excitement, joy, and sadness in email. Remember to avoid all caps and all lowercase wording. Our next chapter will give you even more ideas on how to turn your seemingly boring text format into something creative.

CHAPTER 12

YOUR EMAIL VOICE

> **#1: DON'T** *be a victim of the emotionless email.*

You've got the subject headers, grammar, and everything else down pat. But can people understand your true voice from your email? Are you witty? Are you serious? Think about how you want to come across in emails and how you don't want to come across, and then see how words with "your voice" can come through your emails.

Remember that you want people to want to receive and read your emails. Think about it: You never want to be ignored in person. That goes for your email correspondence, too. So if you feel like being funny, go ahead and brighten someone's day. If you have some serious news to impart or a solemn statement to make, say it in your own respectful style.

At this stage in the evolution of email, don't assume that your recipient has the same email system or the same formatting capabilities as you. It's prudent to assume that most people have basic, no-frills email systems. Your recipient often cannot read your bold, underlined, or italicized text. This section will explore creative ways to use text when text is your only option.

I'M ASLEEP

Subject: Jim is on board

Hello Everyone,

Welcome to Jim Sands, our new project manager. He started today and is located in John's old cubicle.

Thanks,
The Management

This is so boring. What is Jim like? Where does he come from? What does he like to do when he isn't slaving away at the office? Is there a way to give us some insight into Jim as a person? After all, we're going to be working with the guy.

SAME OLD, SAME OLD

Subject: Meeting @ 4

Hello All,

Join us in the meeting room for the weekly conference call with the client to discuss the Star Herald stories.

Fred

I know we have this meeting every week, but I am so not looking forward to it. Can't Fred get a little excited about it and pump up the crew? And, is the Star Herald a newspaper?

NEW KID ON THE BLOCK

Subject: Promotions

Hello to the Jazz Team:

Cindy has been promoted to lead choreographer. She will start immediately. Congratulations to Cindy and thanks to all who tried out for the position.

Thanks,
Jed

Wake me up when it's over.

Is it on-line or online?

Both are acceptable, although online without the hyphen is more common.

> **#1: DO** *let your "voice" be heard*
> *in your emails.*

E-Guidelines For Sharing Your Voice

We have touched on the importance of using your "voice" in your emails. There are a few technical things to remember when creating and sending an email, such as spelling and grammar, which we have covered. But how do you show emotion? And how do you use proper grammar when your email system won't allow you to use italics and other formatting tools such as underlined text?

Here are a few helpful tips.

1. Quotes can double for *italicized text*. For example: "The Miami Herald" is the largest daily newspaper in the metro area.

2. To indicate underlined text, type an underscore before and after the word or phrase you would like underlined. For example: I saw _ Gone With the Wind _ last night for the first time. It was as good as they say.

3. **To indicate bolded text,** type an asterisk (*) before and after the word or phrase you would like bolded, or that you would like to stand out. For example: I want you to know that the *first-ever guide* to complete email communications is now in bookstores.

Emotions: Use Emoticons

In more casual office settings, many people are using emoticons, a word derived by pairing emotion and icon. Emoticons are visual ways of expressing your emotions via email. Without emoticons, it might be difficult for the recipient to know if you are pleased, serious, or disappointed from the tone of your words. Try to send a smile if you are in fact smiling or happy :-).

It's important to keep up with today's e-speak. (See the glossary for more emoticons.) Check with your office manager to see if emoticons are acceptable in your place of work. With regard to sending emoticons to others outside of the office, it's a judgment call. Recipients who have never used emoticons themselves may be confused by them; don't sacrifice clarity for being cute. If your recipients are ultraconservative, it's best not to send the ;-) wink their way just yet.

International Emails

For international emails, you might wonder if others can read your tildes (~) or umlauts (¨). Oftentimes the recipient's email software cannot translate different character sets. Check with your system administrator for ways to handle the differences.

When referring to legal cases, how do I abbreviate the word versus?

Use v. (the letter v and a period) to denote versus. If you are writing the name of an actual case, remember to use italicized text: *Roe v. Wade* or "Roe v. Wade" or underlined text: <u>Roe v. Wade</u> or _Roe v. Wade_.

Time Constraints

What happens when someone has 375 emails to sort through? How will your message get noticed? There never seems to be enough time to do everything, let alone read or respond to all of your email. How can you make the time to make the emails you send *interesting*? Get yourself into a routine. Remember to tell yourself that email communication is *different* than any other form of communication. Establishing your unique voice can be as simple as using a word that you use when you speak, such as "mess hall" for the company's cafeteria. If you are introducing yourself on email, feel free to use your own style, or words you would use when introducing yourself in person, such as "I am friendly, open to suggestions, and always hungry, so we can meet over lunch anytime." With careful planning, your emails can really click.

NEW BEGINNINGS

Subject: It's a long way from Kansas for Jim!

Hello All,

Jim Sands clicked his heels three times and landed here in Washington. He is excited about starting as our new project manager. We are convinced he will be the best project manager we have ever had! All right, so Jim's the first project manager we've ever had. :-).

We are pleased to have Jim with us. Please give him a warm welcome when you see him in our offices today.

Thanks,
The Management

I can't wait to meet the new guy.

TEA TIME

Subject: Cocktails at four

Dear Team,

We will have our weekly conference call with the client today at 4 p.m. The subject of today's call is the cocktail hour that the client is planning for distributors, other CEOs, and local media.

Can't wait to see you there!

Always looking for ways to liven up the party,

Fred

Maybe the weekly meeting won't be so bad after all.

My email software is not able to underline words. And even if it could, I understand many other software programs would not even be able to read it. How do I denote a word or phrase that should be underlined?

To denote an underlined portion of your email, use an _(underscore) before and after the word or phrase you want underlined_. Everything enclosed in the underscore marks should be considered as underlined text.

NEWS, NEWS, NEWS

Subject: Share her joy

Dear All,

Please join me in congratulating Cindy for landing the position as lead choreographer. She's filled with wonderful ideas that will bring our troupe much more attention during our national tour.

I thank all of you who also interviewed. All of you were wonderful. :-) Thanks for your enthusiasm. I will look for ways for all of you to move forward in the near future.

Thanks,
Jed

That is a nice way of showing your enthusiasm.

Your voice is yours and only yours. Experiment with the features on your email system, and give in to your personality. Let it show in your emails. Incorporate emoticons when appropriate. Remember to include the special denotations such as _underlined text_ and you will be sending good vibrations out to the world not only in person, but now over email.

Should the phrase "so-called" be separated by quotes or written in italics?

No, so-called itself is sufficient.

CHAPTER 13

SAMPLE EMAILS THAT CLICK

So there you are, feeling proud of and secure in your new position in the business world. Then your boss asks you to announce the urgent staff meeting via email, and suddenly you feel a panic attack coming on. You can think of a dozen ways to do this, but you can't come up with the right wording.

It has happened to all of us. We have written hundreds of thank you notes, but when it's an email, many of us are stumped! Many people feel awkward with this new communication format.

We believe that most messages or announcements can be sent by email, and that your voice and personality can be heard through your words.

The following sample emails are a selection of the most frequently sent emails in a business setting. Our categories are classic and casual, depending on your office environment. Keep these by your computer, and you will have the correct wording for any office email that you send. Just remember to change the names!

MEETINGS

CLASSIC

File   Edit   Mailbox   Message   Help

Subject: Your participation is requested

To the Staff,

Your participation is requested this Thursday at 3 p.m. in the conference room to discuss future pro bono activities. We will talk about getting more involved as a company with the community.

Everyone's ideas will be appreciated.

Thank you,
Mr. Erickson

CASUAL

File Edit Mailbox Message Help

Subject: You can help

Hi Everyone,

Please join us on Thursday at 3 p.m. in the conference room. We will be talking about pro bono projects for this season. All ideas are welcome!

Thanks,
Jerry

CLASSIC

File Edit Mailbox Message Help

Subject: Important meeting today

To All Staff,

We will have an important meeting this after-noon at 3:30 p.m. in the conference room. Mr. Krause has important news about the IRS. Everyone is required to attend.

Thank you,
Bruce Mac

CASUAL

File   Edit   Mailbox   Message   Help

Subject: Taking on the IRS

Hi Everyone,

We will be having an important meeting at 3:30 p.m. in the conference room. If you would like the scoop about this year's IRS advice, please join us.

See you soon,
Iris

?

What is the difference between justification and ragged right style?

Justification is when the text margins are aligned, and the words are spaced out specifically to meet those exact margins (like this).

Ragged right style is when the right-hand margin is unjustified and line endings vary (like this).

PROMOTIONS

CLASSIC

File Edit Mailbox Message Help

Subject: Sophie Lewis is promoted

Dear Colleagues,

It is my pleasure to announce the promotion of Sophie Lewis to sales manager.

Ms. Lewis began her career with our company in 1998 and has consistently exceeded her goals and yearly quotas. She is a valued asset to our organization. Her new title is effective as of today.

Please join me in congratulating Ms. Lewis.

Sincerely,
Melissa Jones

Can I leave out a period at the end of a sentence if it is obvious that the sentence has ended, such as: "Looking forward to seeing you this afternoon"?

The rules of grammar and style apply to email. Use correct punctuation. Put a period at the end of a sentence.

CASUAL

<u>F</u>ile <u>E</u>dit <u>M</u>ailbox <u>M</u>essage <u>H</u>elp

Subject: Congratulations to Sophie

Hi Everyone,

We are happy to announce that Sophie Lewis has been promoted to sales manager.

Sophie is a great asset to our company and has been a loyal colleague for more than three years. She has demonstrated her ability to improve our business, and we are excited and proud to give her the promotion she deserves. The promotion is effective today.

Congratulations, Sophie!
John

Should I use double spacing or single spacing in my emails?

Use single spacing. If you use at least a 10-point font size, the recipient can generally read it easily. If the email is double-spaced, your recipient might spend too much time scrolling down to read the entire message.

CLASSIC

File Edit Mailbox Message Help

Subject: Zachary Lee is new vice president

To the Staff:

We are proud to announce the promotion of Zachary Lee to vice president.

Mr. Lee has been with the company for five years and has consistently demonstrated his outstanding ability in the field of advertising. His new title is effective March 1.

Sincerely,
Rachel Roth

CASUAL

File Edit Mailbox Message Help

Subject: Congratulations to Zack!

To Everyone,

Please join me in congratulating Zachary Lee on his well-deserved promotion to vice president of the company. Zack will begin his new position on March 1.

Best of luck!

Cheers,
Rachel

ANNOUNCEMENTS

CLASSIC

File Edit Mailbox Message Help

Subject: New policy

Dear Employees,

Please be prepared to show your ID badge
when you enter the building. Every employee
is required to do so. This will be the standard
procedure effective Monday morning.

Thank you,
Mr. Jones

CASUAL

File Edit Mailbox Message Help

Subject: Your security

Dear Staff,

For your security, we will begin requiring
every person to show an ID badge when
entering the building. This routine will begin
on Monday morning. Any questions? Please
let me know.

Thanks for your cooperation,
Andy

CLASSIC

File   Edit   Mailbox   Message   Help

Subject: Painting crews

To Everyone,

We are happy to announce that we are having the office painted and redecorated. Please clear off your desks by noon on Friday. We will begin painting over the weekend.

Thank you for your cooperation,
Ann Jenkins

CASUAL

File   Edit   Mailbox   Message   Help

Subject: New colors!

Hi Everyone,

Good news! We are painting the office this weekend. Please clear off your desks by noon on Friday, and we will take care of the rest.

When you come in on Monday, you will see a bright new office.

Thanks,
Ann

SOCIAL EVENTS

CLASSIC

File Edit Mailbox Message Help

Subject: Happy hour

To Everyone,

We will be having a Happy Hour at the Seven Seas Inn this evening at 6 p.m. Everyone is invited to attend. We will have several designated drivers.

Please let me know if you will be there.

Sincerely,
Daphne

CASUAL

File Edit Mailbox Message Help

Subject: Fun city!

To the Staff:

Please come to Happy Hour tonight at the Seven Seas Inn. The fun will start at 6 p.m., and everyone is invited. If you will be joining us, please let me know.

We will have a few designated drivers.

Cheers,
Ellen

CLASSIC

File   Edit   Mailbox   Message   Help

Subject: Company picnic

To the Staff:

Our annual company picnic will be held this year at the Greenery on Saturday, June 4, from 3–6 p.m. The sign-up sheet for games is in the conference room.

Everyone's participation is encouraged. Please let me know if you will be attending by COB this Friday.

Thank you,
Lillian

How do I determine capitalization of geographic areas?

If the geographical term denotes a place or region, capitalize it. If it denotes a direction, do not capitalize it. For example: Microsoft is in the West or the western United States.

CASUAL

File Edit Mailbox Message Help

Subject: Fun in the sun

Hi Everyone,

We will be having our annual office picnic on
Saturday, June 4, from 3–6 p.m. It will be at
The Greenery, the same location as last year's
blast! We will have games and lots of great
food.

Please let me know if you will be there. The
more the merrier.

Cheers,
Sara

DEPARTURES

CLASSIC

File   Edit   Mailbox   Message   Help

Subject: Greg Ross

Dear Colleagues,

It is with regret that I inform you that our senior vice president, Greg Smith, will be leaving the company. He is starting his own production company in France. Friday will be his last day here.

Greg has always been an asset to us, and we will miss him. We wish him luck and all the best wishes in his pursuits.

Sincerely,
Mike Smith

CASUAL

File   Edit   Mailbox   Message   Help

Subject: Greg's last day

Hi Everyone,

We're not saying good-bye to Greg Ross—just
so long for now. Greg is returning to France to
start his own company. His last day will be on
Friday the 14th. Greg, in addition to being our
vice president, you were also the social chair-
man, and we will miss your poolside parties!

We wish you all the best.

Thanks,
Mike

CLASSIC

File   Edit   Mailbox   Message   Help

Subject: My departure

Dear Staff,

It's been a great three years working with all
of you. Thank you for the wonderful experience. I am opening a new flower shop on
Connecticut Avenue; so please stop by if you
get the chance.

Fond wishes,
Janet

CASUAL

File   Edit   Mailbox   Message   Help

Subject: Janet blossoms

Hi Everyone,

Janet Harris will be leaving our company to start her own flower shop. Janet has been a wonderful asset to our company, and we will miss her. Her last day will be this Friday.

Please join me in wishing Janet lots of success in her new venture.

Cheers,
Ellen

Is it acceptable to abbreviate dates in my emails, such as 5-1-01?

Because we conduct business internationally more and more, it is best to stay away from abbreviated dates. To an American, 5-1-01 is May 1, 2001. To the British, however, it is 5 January 2001. Acceptable forms for dates are either May 1, 2001 (American style) or 1 May 2001 (European style).

URGENT EMAILS

CLASSIC

File Edit Mailbox Message Help

Subject: URGENT MESSAGE

To the Staff:

Your attendance is required at the company-wide staff meeting this afternoon at 3:30 p.m. Our board of directors will be expecting everyone to be present.

To make certain everyone is notified, we will also leave voice-mail messages and make personal visits.

Your attendance is important to the well-being of our organization!

Sincerely,
Mr. Price

What is the correct spelling: floppy disk or floppy disc?

Floppy disk. Disc is most often used in connection with compact discs (CDs).

CASUAL

File Edit Mailbox Message Help

Subject: Urgent meeting

To Everyone,

We will be having an urgent meeting at 3:30 p.m. today. Our board of directors is in town, and your attendance is expected. Please don't let us down.

We will also leave voice mails and make personal visits to everyone concerned.

See you there,
Robert

CLASSIC

File Edit Mailbox Message Help

Subject: URGENT MESSAGE TO EVERYONE

Dear Staff,

If you have any files or information regarding the Smith account, please let me know immediately. I need everything you might possibly have by 10 a.m. tomorrow. This is important.

Please reply to this email, whether you have information or not. We appreciate your help.

Thank you,
Mr. Stubbs

CASUAL

File   Edit   Mailbox   Message   Help

Subject: Urgent information needed!

To Everyone,

Please let me know if you have any files or memos from the Smith account. We need to have this information by 10 a.m. tomorrow. If you have notes or information you think could help us, please let me know ASAP!

This is very important to our team.

Thanks,
Ray

What is text format?

Text format is a simple, universal form of type that most computers can use to communicate with one another. Also called ASCII, it is not capable of specialized formatting such as bold, italic, or different font styles. Most email systems use this text format because they all can read and understand it.

THANK YOU NOTES

CLASSIC

File   Edit   Mailbox   Message   Help

To: Janice Updike
From: Carol Franklin
Re: Thank you for lunch

Dear Janice,

Thank you for the lunch at The Carlton today. It was a pleasure to catch up with you outside of the office, and I enjoyed hearing about your boat trip to the Galápagos. Donald and I are thinking now of going ourselves!

I look forward to reciprocating the favor soon.

Thanks again,
Carol

CASUAL

File   Edit   Mailbox   Message   Help

Hey Janice,

It was great to see you today at The Carlton. Thanks for a wonderful lunch, and I can't wait to catch up with you again soon. After hearing about your trip to the Galápagos, I'm dying to go now, too!

Take care,
Carol

CLASSIC

File Edit Mailbox Message Help

To: Kate Misty
From: Alice Reirdon
Re: Thank you

Dear Kate,

Thank you for the compliment today. I feel much more encouraged about the environmental project after speaking with you.

Looking forward to finishing up soon!

Many thanks,
Alice

CASUAL

File Edit Mailbox Message Help

Re: Thanks for the pick-me-up!

Dear Kate,

Thanks for the encouragement today. I enjoyed the pep talk and am pumped about finishing the environmental project. We'll have to go out for drinks when this is all over.

Thanks,
Alice

LUNCH INVITATION

CLASSIC

File   Edit   Mailbox   Message   Help

To: Jayne Shaw
From: Cristi Barnett
Re: Lunch on Friday

Dear Jayne,

Are you free for lunch on Friday? I think it would be a good idea to go over the month-end report out of the office. How about the GHQ Restaurant at noon?

Please RSVP me by COB tomorrow, so I can make a reservation. Thanks.

Best,
Cristi

CASUAL

File   Edit   Mailbox   Message   Help

Re: Lunch on me!

How about lunch at the GHQ at noon Friday? Please drop me a note by the end of the day tomorrow so I can make reservations.

Thanks,
Carolyn

CLASSIC

File   Edit   Mailbox   Message   Help

To: Book Club Members
From: Kirstie Crawford
Re: Book club member lunch

Please join us:
Who: Book Club Members
What: Our monthly lunch
Where: Battery Park
When: July 1, Noon

Please RSVP to Kirstie at kirstie@dot.com

Thanks,
Kirstie

CASUAL

File   Edit   Mailbox   Message   Help

To: Book Club Members
From: Kirstie Crawford
Re: Book club member lunch

Dear All,

Please join us for lunch in Battery Park on July 1. We will meet at the usual place at noon. We plan to discuss our fall charity book sale.

See you there,

Kirstie

NEW CLIENT

CLASSIC

File Edit Mailbox Message Help

To: Nina, Kathy, Kristine
From: Jim
Re: New Client: France!

Dear Nina, Kathy, and Kristine,

The Government of France is our new client!
Congratulations on all of your hard work
preparing the proposal. The client was im-
pressed by our track record, our ideas for the
2001 budget, and our sense of team spirit.

Thanks for a job well done,
Jim

What is a page break?

A page break is the end of a page, either set
automatically by word processing software
or adjusted manually by the writer.

CASUAL

<u>F</u>ile <u>E</u>dit <u>M</u>ailbox <u>M</u>essage <u>H</u>elp

To: Nina, Kathy, Kristine
From: Jim
Re: Vive la France!

Good news!

The Government of France has hired us. After two years of negotiations, we have come to an agreement. Thanks for your dedication in making this happen.

Please join me tonight at 6 p.m. at the Jefferson Hotel for a celebratory drink.

Cheers,
Jim

Why is email so valuable in business communications today?

Email is a quick, easy, and cost-effective mode of communication. It is also a great and easy way to save all correspondences, sent and received.

CLASSIC

File   Edit   Mailbox   Message   Help

To: The A-Team
From: Judy Mohler
Re: New client

Hello to the A-Team:

Our newest client is Tree Industries, a recycling company. We will be Tree's consulting firm for the next year. The retainer fee is $30,000 per month plus expenses.

As department head, I thought you would be pleased to include these figures in our projections. I will also announce the good news globally.

Thank you,
Reggie

What is gothic print?

Gothic print is another term for block letters, or a print without any style.

CASUAL

File   Edit   Mailbox   Message   Help

Re: Tree huggers unite!

Congratulations to all of you for for helping to land our newest client, Tree Industries. We will be Tree's consulting firm for the next year. The retainer fee is $30,000 per month plus expenses.

As department head, I thought you would be pleased to include these figures in our projections. I will also announce the good news globally.

Thanks,
Reggie

What is the correct spelling: "program" or "programme"?

Stick to American English, if that is the English you know: program. Like anything else, be consistent.

ANNIVERSARY

CLASSIC

File Edit Mailbox Message Help

To: Global Staff
From: Matthew Sherry
Re: Office anniversaries this month

Our office anniversaries are as follows for the month of December:

1 — Ann Anselmi
7 — June O'Connell
15 — Mary Muoio
18 — Eve Brown
19 — Jane Placko
22 — Marilyn Moore

Congratulations to all!

Thanks,
Matthew

CASUAL

File   Edit   Mailbox   Message   Help

Re: Anniversaries o' the month

Please join me in congratulating all of those who have anniversaries this month.

1 — Ann Anselmi
7 — June O'Connell
15 — Mary Muoio
18 — Eve Brown
19 — Jane Placko
22 — Marilyn Moore

A special congrats goes to June O'Connell on her 25-year anniversary with the company.

You are all wonderful assets to our company!

Best wishes,
Matthew

CLASSIC

<u>F</u>ile <u>E</u>dit <u>M</u>ailbox <u>M</u>essage <u>H</u>elp

To: Ned
From: Ginny
Re: Your anniversary

Dear Ned,

Congratulations on your 10-year anniversary with the company. You are the most productive employee I have ever had on my staff, and it is a privilege to work with you.

To celebrate your decade with the company, I would like to take you to lunch today at the Art Gallery Grille. Are you free at noon?

Thanks again for your remarkable work.

Best,
Ginny

CASUAL

File Edit Mailbox Message Help

To: Ned
From: Ginny
Re: Your anniversary

Dear Ned,

Happy anniversary to you! Happy anniversary to you! Happy anniversary to Ned...Happy anniversary to you!

This means it is review time, so how about talking together on Friday? It is time for a promotion and a raise! Our ad agency would fall apart without you.

Congratulations,
Ginny

EVENTS IN OFFICE

CLASSIC

File Edit Mailbox Message Help

To: All Staff
From: Anjan Shah
Re: Halloween

Dear Halloween Fans:

WHO: All Staff
WHAT: Halloween costume party contest
WHERE: Our conference room
WHEN: Halloween, noon

Prizes for costumes include:
Best Overall Costume: Dinner for two at the restaurant of your choice
Scariest Costume: Two tickets to an NHL or NBA game locally
Funniest Costume: $20 gift certificate at Dickey's
Prettiest Costume: $10 gift certificate at Brewood Engravers
Worst Costume: Nothing but a bad reputation

Looking forward to seeing you there.

Thanks,
Anjan

CASUAL

File Edit Mailbox Message Help

To: All Staff
From: Anjan Shah
Re: Ghosts and goblins!

Dear Halloween Revelers:

Guess what's happening on October 31 in our office?

A party!

Please join us for the annual Halloween party and costume contest in the meeting room today at noon.

The categories and corresponding prizes for the contest this year are as follows:
Best Overall Costume: Dinner for two at the restaurant of your choice
Scariest Costume: Two tickets to an NHL or NBA game locally
Funniest Costume: $20 gift certificate at Dickey's
Prettiest Costume: $10 gift certificate at Brewood Engravers
Worst Costume: Nothing but a bad reputation

What are you going to be?

Looking forward to seeing you there.

Thanks,
Anjan

CLASSIC

File   Edit   Mailbox   Message   Help

To: Gabby, Jerry, Martha, Victoria, Sandy, and Isabella
From: Rebecca
Re: Memorial service for Ralph

Hello All,

For those of you who would like to gather for a moment of silence in memory of Ralph, please join us in my office tomorrow at 5 p.m. for 30 minutes or so. Feel free to bring and share any thoughts or words.

Sincerely,
Rebecca

CASUAL

File   Edit   Mailbox   Message   Help

Re: Memorial service for Ralph, our friend

Dear All,

Please join me in celebrating the life of a beloved colleague and friend, Ralph. We will join together this afternoon in my office at 3 p.m.

Yours,
Rebecca

EVENTS OUT OF OFFICE

CLASSIC

File Edit Mailbox Message Help

To: San Diego Office Staff
From: Tina Urbanski
Re: Party — RSVP

Dear Staff,

Our annual company summer party will be next month. Here are the details. Please RSVP if you can attend, and indicate how many will be in your party, including family members.

What: Company Party
Where: The Grounds
When: 1–5 p.m., July 1

Things to do for the whole family: moon walk, softball, BBQ, open bar. Casual dress. Please RSVP and ask for directions if you need them.

Thanks,
Tina

CASUAL

File Edit Mailbox Message Help

Dear All,

Re: Open bar, moon walk...who could ask for more?

Who: You and the family
What: Family Day Event
Where: The Rialto Park
When: 1–3 p.m., Saturday, July 5

Come and have fun with us.

Cheers,
Ed

What should I do if I receive an email with an attachment from someone I do not know? Or from a familiar email address, but the email reads something odd, like, "Open this. This is cool."

Do not open the attachment and delete the file immediately. By running the attachment, you may infect yourself with any number of computer viruses, which are frequently transmitted through attached files. See chapter 14.

CLASSIC

File Edit Mailbox Message Help

Re: Holiday party

Distinguished colleagues,

Who: The San Francisco office
What: Holiday party event
When: December 15
Where: The Palm, 7–9 p.m.

Please join us! We will celebrate the holidays together and reflect on a wonderful year for our company.

Please RSVP by COB Friday.

Best wishes from your office manager,
Ronnie

CASUAL

File   Edit   Mailbox   Message   Help

Re: Holly, Jolly Christmas

Dear Spirited Colleagues: (sung to the tune of
"Jingle Bells")

Dashing through the snow,
On a corporate engine sleigh
To Sam and Harry's we go
Laughing all the way
Friday, December 15, we'll go,
Making spirits bright
To drink and eat and sing and dance
We'll do it at six o'clock that night!
Ohhh... jingle bells, jingle bells...

RSVP to me by December 10.

Best wishes,
Ronnie

Keep this sample emails chapter marked in your book;
it can be a good point of reference for you when you have to
quickly write a thank you note or anniversary email, for instance. Most importantly, create your own voice by tailor-
ing these emails to your personality, while always keeping
your audience, classic or casual, in mind.

CHAPTER 14

DON'T LET THE EMAIL BUGS BITE

VIRUSES AND SECURITY ON EMAIL

A growing area of concern with email is security. Many people in the business world are justifiably afraid of hackers getting into and stealing or destroying their files, or of the multitude of nasty viruses spreading across the globe. Just like our bodies are not immune to various viruses, our computers are also vulnerable to attack by new viruses for which they have no defenses. But we can take precautions. Just as we eat right, get the proper amount of sleep, and exercise in order to stay strong and healthy to ward off viruses that attack the human body, we need to take similar preventative precautions with our computers.

This chapter outlines crucial defenses that you should use to protect yourself as best as you possibly can from security hazards.

Delete Suspicious Email Attachments

If you receive an email with an attachment from someone you do not know, be wary. When in doubt, delete the email immediately. Make sure you delete the attached file, too. In many email systems, the attachments automatically go to a default directory on the hard drive, and you'll need to use your file manager to find the file and delete it without opening it. Then go to your recycle bin and empty it. Sure, you might delete an innocent message that you would not have deleted had you known its contents, but it just isn't worth the risk of potentially losing all the data on your computer to a virus.

In any case, if you see that the filename of the attachment ends in ".exe" or ".vbs," delete the email right away. These are generally viruses or other executable files that need only DOS/Windows to run. Then there are those that need a specific application, such as MS Word (ending in ".doc") or MS Excel (ending in ".xls") to execute. Viruses are spread most commonly through executable attachments, such as these, rather than through plain text documents, usually ending in ".txt." Other files, ending in ".shs," are also harmful, but they can hide their identity, appearing as ".txt" files, much like a Trojan Horse that hides its deadly contents behind a harmless facade. The "I Love You" virus spread throughout the world in the form of a ".vbs" attachment. That particular virus needed two conditions to work: people opening the attachment, and the Windows operating system, which would allow the virus to run. Once the virus made its way into computer systems, it sent emails containing copies of itself to everyone in the infected computers' email address books. Those people who did not open the email attachment did not get the virus.

Viruses Can Come From Email Addresses You Know

Even if you receive an email with an attachment from someone you know, if the attached file has any of the executable files mentioned above delete it immediately. Or, if it reads, "Open this. This is cool," for example, above an executable file, be wary. Doesn't she, the sender, usually start her emails with "Hey, Mojo" when writing to you? And, she always signs her initials at the end of her emails, "KRM." Neither references are on this email. You should be suspicious. Games and other visual attachments are popular targets for viruses because people love to play games, and the viruses are almost

---

What is a hard copy and why is it important?

A hard copy is a printout of something that has been stored on computer. It is always good to make a hard copy or printout of a document or file in case of damage to the computer. In some cases of damage, files may not be retrievable.

always introduced by vague and impersonal messages. Carefully review emails before opening attachments, even from someone you know. They may be an unwitting accomplice who was also a target of the same virus. Your time spent playing a game attachment is valuable corporate time. It could also wreak company-wide havoc. Save yourself some time: delete it.

How Are Viruses Born?

Virus writers are fundamentally malicious people who often want as many people as possible to see of what they are capable. The writers find a security flaw in a software program and then start sending the virus around. The virus finds various ways to enter your system: through an executable email attachment, the network, or downloads. Once it runs, the virus finds its way to your hard drive, and once there, it can use your files to wreak havoc on your computer and its data. Microsoft is a common target for many virus writers, because its software is the most ubiquitous. The virus writers know that by penetrating Microsoft security flaws, and spreading their viruses through MS users, they can reach the largest number of people. As long as there are mean people in the world, unfortunately, there will be viruses, and even the mutations that viruses create. See www.symantec.com for more interesting information about viruses.

Downloading From The Internet

You have heard the horror stories about downloading software programs from the Internet. You may have even downloaded some yourself. Didn't your system administrator at work send you emails urging you not to download items from the Internet? The Internet offers so many great features, games, and other exciting downloaded files, but just download from sites you trust. Big software companies usually are safe and have "authentication" keys, such as www.verisign.com, for your protection. You can set your Internet browser to "secure settings," which will warn you before downloading potentially unsafe content. For example, when using Internet Explorer, choose Tools then Internet Options then Security to set this up. Any download can have a virus attached to it that will spread like wildfire through your system, and perhaps that of your entire network. It is usually safe to download helpful information and "tools" or "utilities," however, from your own company or other software companies, such as antivirus companies, whose interest is protecting its users and other consumers.

Hand-Held Technology

Another area of growing concern is viruses affecting gadgets that utilize wireless technology, such as the Palm Pilot and cellular telephone. The most sophisticated versions allow you to have more interactivity with the outside world. As new technology makes our lives more convenient, the more opportunities hackers will find to create their bugs. In the '90s, the big threat to computer systems was through tainted disks and disk drives. Think about how easily one could clean the targeted disk or disk drive, erase the virus, and stop it dead in its tracks. The viruses spread slowly, and it was easy to eradicate them. Today, with viruses traveling by email, it is harder to combat viruses that spread at the speed of light through global data networks that connect an ever-growing percentage of the world population.

Preventative Measures

We have developed a few guidelines to follow that will help you to avoid viruses:

→ Remember to exercise your practical judgment. Don't open attachments that look suspicious. Some people will open an attachment only when they know in advance that it's coming, and from whom.

→ Install up-to-date antivirus software to protect your computer. Some software packages screen your system right after you turn on your computer, before you begin to run programs. If it finds a virus, the program can clean it up for you. Companies such as Norton (www.norton.com) and McAfee (www.mcafee.com) make antivirus software and have helpful protective information on their Web sites. Another helpful site is www.complex.is/f-prof.com. You may also download the latest antivirus technology from their sites.

→ Keep up with the latest news about viruses. Which ones are out there? How are they affecting programs? Visit the Norton and McAffee sites, which will keep you informed. Microsoft's Tech Net has current information on viruses at www.microsoft.com/technet/security/.

→ Always have a password set up on your computer, and perhaps even a separate one for your email system, to prevent security breaches from outside of your physical hardware.

→ Do not download from the Internet unless you are assured it is a secure site.

→ Develop a good rapport with people whom you regularly email. When sending email attachments, it is best to tell the recipient ahead of time what information is coming in the attachment. Also include the filename and what application (with version) it was created in. It is always good form to let a busy person know to look out for an email.

What To Do If You Run The Virus

Turn off your computer immediately. Don't shut down the computer as you normally would. Simply push the power button off. Call your system administrator or your software company immediately. The key is to solve the problem quickly so it doesn't spread network-wide. Perhaps you didn't run the file but you have already saved the virus on your hard drive. In that case, you can delete the file just as you would any other.

CHAPTER 15

LOOK WHO'S EMAILING

We asked the experts to define the most important aspects of emails, ranging from etiquette to business to legal to academic viewpoints. Here are the answers to our questions:

Thank You Notes

Business protocol expert and former social secretary to First Lady Jacqueline Kennedy, Letitia Baldrige, told us, "It's perfectly acceptable to send thank you notes by email, especially for lunch or a meeting." For more formal occasions, such as a museum dinner or a client wedding, Baldrige recommends the old-fashioned handwritten thank you note. We agree. Go email!

To make your life easier, save a "bread and butter" thank you note as a template in your email filing system, so that you can get those notes out quickly to people. For instance:

Dear Miles,

Thank you for the kind career advice.
Will take you up on it!

Best,
Steven

Sounds simple enough? However, most of us dread finding the pen and stationery to put together this note. Remember to save time and stress. Email it. This method is quick, cost-effective, and thoughtful.

Legal Questions

In a conversation with U.S. Attorney General Janet Reno, she reminded us that the Internet is not just in your neighborhood, but it crosses international borders. (Think "Love Bug.") When sending emails to business contacts in other countries, we have to remember that the laws of our country might not apply abroad. According to Reno, "the biggest problem in the near future is going to be how we coordinate the various legal systems around the world. If the U.S. identifies an Internet or email perpetrator in another country, and he or she is immune through that country's laws, then we are going to have problems." Reno is determined to rally the countries of the world together to create a joint law governing the Internet and email. Don't Stub Your Pinkie Overseas might be our follow-up book in this case!

Are digital signatures legal? In other words, are deals made over the Internet with no handwritten signatures legal? Yes, they are now. The so-called E-sign Act was signed into law by President Bill Clinton on June 30, 2000, and is paving the way for businesses to thrive on the Internet. Digital signatures are now as legally binding as handwritten ones. In an age where more businesses and consumers are involved in e-commerce, the laws are now reflecting and protecting this booming industry. Passwords, electronic thumbprints, and other features will help to keep consumers safe from foul play.

The Diplomatic Corps

In diplomatic circles, certain international audiences use more formal language on email. Know your audience. Gail Scott, author of *Diplomatic Dance: The New Embassy Life in America*, says the diplomatic corps—especially the younger ambassadors—is communicating via email. "If an ambassador gives you his or her email address, it is an invitation to use it, not unlike someone giving you their private cell phone number, reserved for family and close friends," says Scott.

However, use it wisely, and remember that many ambassadors hold other titles such as Sir Christopher, the British ambassador. "If you are not already on a first name basis,

---

How should I separate paragraphs in my emails?

Leave an empty line between paragraphs, so the reader can easily see where one paragraph ends and another begins.

always use the proper salutation on email as you would in a letter," says Scott. "Let them *invite* you to use their first name."

The Academic Seers

Why are people sloppy on email? "Because they can be," says Kenneth Brown, assistant professor of management and organizations at the University of Iowa in Iowa City. Brown says people know that they can spend less time creating and sending an email than picking up the telephone to place a call, dialing the number, and going through the voice-mail system, or writing a letter, addressing it, placing a stamp on the envelope, and dropping it off in a mailbox. "Email is fast and easy, and people use it that way," he says.

"It [isn't] the technology that's made for sloppy communication. It's the lack of understanding of it," says Brian Richardson, associate professor of journalism at Washington and Lee University in Lexington, Virginia. "People treat

Do I capitalize "president" when referring to the head of my company?

The word "president" by itself is not capitalized. Capitalize "president" when it is a title that comes before a proper name. For example: I walked beside President Carter at the Habitat for Humanity event. Do not capitalize "president" when it follows the name. For example: Todd Wood, president of Widgetcom, will be the main speaker at the conference.

email as the equivalent of a phone conversation. The feature of almost immediate feedback with email encourages that, making it quite different from other forms of written communication. When we are in a hurry, we tend not to check things or rewrite."

The key is to police yourself. Richardson uses email for approximately 90 percent of his correspondence. "The obvious advantage [of email] is that I no longer have to play telephone tag with people," he says. "For me, there's an irony. While many people decry the spontaneity that email engenders, I like it for the opportunity it gives me for instant send-and-receive technology together with the advantage of policing and revising my message before I send it. Too often in a phone conversation, you've said something before you've thought enough. And there's the problem with 'l'esprit de l'escalier': thinking of what you should have said 30 seconds after you hang up."

Brown sees email as being convenient for colleagues who know each other well. Brown's primary concern with email is that we will use our bad habits from casual email communications in our more formal communications.

What is the future of email communication? Brown says that email is still relatively new and, unlike in other business situations, there is comparatively little training. So more formal training might be increasingly popular in the future.

Richardson says that email communication will increase in the future. "The postal service is passé, except for the most intensely personal or the most formal communications," he says.

"People, however, will begin to police themselves a little more," says Richardson. But take heed. "Email security is about the equivalent of sending a postcard. The recent court cases allowing employers to read employee emails will give people a wake-up call, and cut down on the steamy-letters-to-Bertha that people seem to regard, to their eventual chagrin, as the equivalent of a personal conversation."

The Entrepreneurial Spin

Are people more productive with email?

"If I were a coffee or water cooler supplier, I would not be so excited about the dawn of email," says Tim Foster, president of eSynchronized Marketing, a new company in Bethesda, Maryland. "In many offices, email has replaced the coffee machine and water cooler. At one time these were the places where coworkers could gather around to gossip and discuss their lives. Email makes these gatherings easier than ever and best of all you don't have to leave your desk. Now all you have to do is use instant messaging or email and you are instantly connected to the office buzz.

"Best of all," he says, "your boss, who occasionally passes by sees you diligently typing on your computer and thinks how productive his or her work force has become. The question in my mind is, are we more or less productive because of IM (instant messaging) and email?

"Yes, it's easier to communicate with one another, but how much is too much?" asks Foster. "We all have those friends and coworkers who love to send commercial clips, jokes, rate your mate surveys, etc. You know who I'm talking about. Everybody knows at least one person who seems to forward everything they get to every person in their address book. I always wonder how much more productive these people are because of email.

"Then there are the people who use email to keep in better touch with suppliers and clients. You know, the person who deletes all the 'funny jokes' and forwarded messages because they don't have time to read them. They use the technology to further business relationships. I'm not saying email shouldn't be used for fun, but it's just like any tool—it's only as efficient as the person using it."

Messaging From a Different View

"The email is probably single-handedly responsible for reviving the lost art of written correspondence," says Kolev Dworkin, senior database administrator at AOL. "With the advent of the telephone, pen and paper became the modus communicado of only the terminally literate and the luddite. Email reinvigorated a process that had become archaic in its use of tree and graphite. If the founding fathers were alive today, the Constitution would probably be contained within an office memo issued in an email.

"We are, however, rapidly progressing beyond the simple email. One of the most profound new developments in electronic communication is the instant message (IM). Instant messaging allows its correspondents to type messages to each other in real time as they sit at their respective computer consoles. Instant messaging is to email what the telephone

Do I need a question mark when I write a request? For example: a sentence beginning with: "Can you please..."

No, you do not need a question mark when writing a request. For example: Can you please forward me all of your work by COB. However, a clearer way to express the request is to make it a polite command: Please forward all of your work to me by COB.

was to the telegraph. Instant messaging affords the luxury, the time to think and carefully frame thoughts, that traditionally has been the sole purview of the written word. Verbal nuances and tone have been replaced with happy faces and context. This ability to communicate without voice and yet still experience instantaneous communication is a remarkable change in the way we talk to each other. The telegraph or even Morse code offered these abilities decades ago, but they have never been used by a mass audience nor with such ease. The Pony Express would have been green with envy had they been able to witness the speed with which the written word can now be transmitted and more importantly responded to in kind.

"One of the useful differences between instant messaging and voice is the availability of a conversational history. Every IM conversation is akin to having a personal court stenographer. Gone are the disputes about what was said. One needs only to scroll up to see the entire conversation exactly as it transpired. Enhancements to this technology are coming rapidly; one can now add graphics, and sound, and soon perhaps event scents, to an instant message transforming a written message into a multimedia experience. These developments point to a future where the written word, voice, smell, and maybe even tactile stimulation merge into a form of communication that utilizes all the senses, but at a safe distance."

CHAPTER 16

EMAIL HORROR STORIES

Keep those emails coming in. Visit our Web site at www.dontstubyourpinkie.com with your favorite email horror stories!

All of us who use email have had that "Oh, no!" moment—just after sending an email. You think, "Oh, no! What did I just mistakenly send out?" Or you think, "Did I really just send that risqué email joke to my boss?" Then there are the situations where you really goofed in a number of ways: bad spelling, wrong names, or incorrect information. Email horror stories are becoming topics of conversation around the water cooler and at cocktail parties. We have selected some of our favorite email faux pas stories to pass on to you, accompanied by a corresponding E-TIP to help you turn the "Oh, no's" into "Okays!". These scenarios may seem familiar to you. These are true stories that happened to people we know. We have changed some of the names to avoid public mortification!

Oops!

It happens to us all. Melissa had a COB deadline to deliver a document to her client. She was racing against the clock. She finished just in time, and all she had to do was email the final document to her client. She keys in the email address and writes, "Hi, Brian. Attached is our final document. Please call us with any questions. Best, Melissa." Melissa clicks on SEND and away the email goes. She is relieved and satisfied after a long, hard day of work. She turns off her computer, heads to the subway, and looks forward to a quiet evening at home.

She arrives at home and panic sets in. Suddenly, she realizes that she *forgot to attach the document* to the email! She frantically searches her phone book for the client's phone number and calls him to explain. He is not there, and she has missed her deadline. She will have to either go back to the office or email the document the next day. Oops!

E-TIP: Don't forget to attach documents. If it is an urgent matter, you can attach the document first and then write the cover email. Or tie a string around your finger, tape a note to yourself on your monitor, or devise another technique that will help you remember.

It'll Cost You

Ellen was on a business trip to Seattle. She had 30 minutes until her next meeting, so she went to her hotel room, plugged in her laptop, and logged onto her company server. She discovered 129 new email messages since she checked yesterday! She didn't have time to read all of them before the meeting, so she decided to screen the emails according to the sender's email address and the subject header of the email. For instance, if a message was from her company president and referenced as URGENT, it would certainly go on the "open now" list.

The first email she opened was from her office manager, and it was labeled OFFICE RULES. It might be information about a new policy that could affect her immediately. Instead, it turned out to be a top 10 list of America's funniest office rules. And, on top of that, the list was in the form of an attachment, which took four minutes to upload. Remember Ellen was using long-distance minutes on the hotel's phone lines. All of these "mistaken identity" emails ate up Ellen's precious time and cost the company money.

E-TIP: When you get back to the office, email the office manager and ask him kindly to take you off of his joke list. We don't recommend anyone sending jokes around the office.

It's The Little Things

Julian was pursuing a special prospective client for his travel agency. They had spoken on the phone and via voice mail. They were about to close the new business deal, and the client wanted to be emailed with the proposal.

This prospect was sensitive about details and wanted everything to be perfect for the tour they were about to book. Julian put everything together and emailed the proposal to the address, PEOPLE@IAMAPROSPECTIVECLIENT.COM.

What's wrong with this picture? The client's address was really all lowercase, so the email never reached the client. Julian lost the deal.

E-TIP: Sometimes it's the little details that count most. Check all email addresses before sending out the emails. Most Web sites and email addresses aren't case sensitive, but some may be.

May The Force Be With You

Katrina is a brilliant and creative entrepreneur. Her product line is doing well, and she has a large staff of commissioned sales representatives selling her line. She relies on email to let them know of late-breaking publicity. So when one of her spokespersons had an appearance on the *Today Show*, Katrina was eager to alert her reps. She emailed them detailed information about the interview. After doing so, she forwarded the message to her spokesperson to show her how proud she was of the booking.

Katrina also added a note to this message saying that she hoped the sales reps wouldn't be too lazy and would really work on this opportunity.

You know what happened. Katrina mistakenly clicked on the SEND TO ALL key, and *everyone* received the second email, too. There is nothing worse than a disgruntled sales force.

Good news though. Katrina sent a note of apology to all the sales reps. The spokesperson was a big hit on the show, and the product did well as a result.

E-TIP: Always give the SEND TO space a good look before sending out.

Back To The Future

Flora received an urgent email from her husband, Louis, about a project he was working on. She opened it immediately. One of her husband's editors, who was new to the job, had completely misunderstood the article her husband wrote and was questioning the information. Louis sent the article as an attachment to Flora, and she read the whole thing. She thought the new editor was stupid and emailed back using the REPLY function:

Hi,

This is stupid.

Love,

Flora

But Flora didn't actually email her husband. After she received her husband's email, she opened the attachment, which was itself an email. By clicking REPLY, Flora did not email her husband, who sent her this information, but instead replied to the address on her monitor at that moment—the email address of the editor. Oops!

E-TIP: When responding to emails, make certain your reply goes back to the original sender. If in doubt, play it safe and create a whole new email.

So You Don't Want To Be A Millionaire?

Kevin receives so many emails every day that he deletes any email without a subject header. That's how he missed a great opportunity. When the board of directors of his company voted to expand its services and include an online electronic sales division, the company extended an initial public offering (IPO) to help fund the new venture.

The company president placed the IPO on the company's email the next morning, among other venues. In the excitement of the moment, however, she forgot to include a subject header. Kevin received the "no header" email and, figuring that opening that particular email was a waste, he and many of his colleagues hit the DELETE key.

The IPO, offered at 10 cents per share, closed with few takers. Six months later, it was listed on the NASDAQ at $8 a share. This was a once-in-a-lifetime opportunity that didn't click!

E-TIP: Never assume that a no-subject email is automatic cyberwaste.

Control Yourself

Once in a while, we all get irritated in the office. Occasionally, we might even vent our frustrations on others. That's what Susan did when she discovered her secretary had accidentally deleted all of the client files on the computer system. Susan sent a nasty email, which included a lot of "x$%&*" profane language. The next day Susan calmed down and realized her email was way out of line. She apologized to her secretary, but it was too late. The secretary had forwarded the email rantings to human resources, and now Susan is on probation for mistreating an employee.

E-TIP: Take an anger management class, but don't vent your frustrations over email. You will regret it. On a related note, if someone emails you a mean message, do not respond. You don't want to stoop to their level. Best advice is to work it out verbally. Don't start a paper trail that you will later regret.

For Whom The Bell Tolls

Amy was hard at work at the office when her email system received an incoming message, signaled with a "ding" sound like that of a bell. It was an email from her college pal, and it was labeled, "News." Excited to hear from her friend Angela, Amy immediately opened the message, which was addressed to Amy and 10 other girlfriends from college.

Should I write numbers in their numeral form, or spell them out?

This is handled in different ways in different types of publications. For example, newspaper style is to spell out whole numbers one to nine and use figures for anything 10 and higher. Book style, on the other hand, spells out numbers from one to a hundred. Business communication often uses newspaper style.

Angela wrote that her brother, Jed, had been gunned down while at an ATM machine. Amy knew Jed well and began to cry. She was so upset that she couldn't work for the rest of the day.

E-TIP: You might want to share bad news on the telephone, or at least via a home email address. This is not an appropriate message to send to your friend's work email address.

Bridges Burned

Robert was happy to leave his old career in human resources for a new job in a law firm. Robert had chaffed under the human resources department's insistence that employees be politically correct at all times. He announced his new position to friends in seven separate emails.

When one of Robert's friends from his old office emailed him back, Robert closed the message and saved it, with the intention of responding to it later. An hour later, Robert clicked on the message in his mailbox and opened it again. He clicked REPLY and wrote an informal yet scathing email. The recipient was his pal after all. Why not be candid? Robert said he was so glad to be away from the old office, and far away from all of those "stiffs" in it.

He clicked on REPLY and off it went—to his former boss. Robert misread the original email address in his mailbox. His friend and boss had similar email addresses: roberts@theoldcompany.com (the boss) and robinson@theoldcompany.com (the friend).

The boss emailed Robert back and said that everyone in the office was glad to see Robert out of the H.R. line of work. So much for asking his old boss for a future recommendation!

E-TIP: Nasty emails can come back to haunt you.

That's None Of Your Business

Sissy invited the office to happy hour. One of her colleagues, Janie, replied by sending an email to the entire office, recapping the last happy hour: "Count me in, Sissy! Remember last happy hour when we met those law students and partied all night with them? We were so wasted. Let's go all out again tonight!"

E-TIP: Change your mindset and do not use that reply all feature unless you absolutely must.

Almost A Miss

Finishing up her last weeks of an internship, Jessica was looking for full-time employment. She logged on to her emails and found there were 50. She started sorting—deleting all emails that looked like junk, based on the subject header; a few forwarded jokes from the receptionist; and some mail from addresses she didn't recognize. Then one of the emails with an unfamiliar address caught her eye; the subject header read, "The message you were waiting for." Jessica's first reaction was "Oh, no, some pervert has my work email address." She was about to delete the email when she decided to open it and see what it was about. The email, as it turns out, was from someone who interviewed her for a job, although the interviewer was using his home address, which she didn't recognize. He was offering her a job! This truly was the message she had been waiting for! Good thing she hesitated on the delete button.

E-TIP: Be careful how you label your emails. Fun subject headers are cute, but sometimes they are misinterpreted. And, think twice before deleting your emails so quickly.

You'll Catch A Cold

Rafaela was in Budapest for three years and came back to the States a new woman—happy and more worldly. She started working in a job in Seattle. She brought computer files from her former office with her, saved on disk. Upon arrival at the new job, she saved many of her disk files to the computer hard drive, which was networked to the entire office. A virus attached to one of her documents immediately corrupted the system. A warning flashed on her computer screen. She didn't think to call the system administrator at the time. She then proceeded to send one of the corrupted documents via email to one of the company's vendors. The vendor opened the attachment, and then the virus was transferred to his system as well. What a way to start the new job! The system administrator was finally called to the rescue.

E-TIP: Be careful to make sure that the documents you send over email are not corrupted. On the receiving end, do not open attachments if you don't know the sender. If you do know the sender, still take precautions. Ask your system administrator how to handle attachments.

CHAPTER 17

YOUR VOICE OF THE FUTURE TODAY

Email gives you a chance to create a new image for yourself. When you answer the telephone, do you sometimes soften your voice? Or do you add an extra professional tone to the way you talk on the telephone? With email, you can create even more of your own personal touch. But remember to start now. You know how important first impressions can be.

We realize your life is busy, but if you make your emails interesting, your clients and colleagues will open *your* emails first. They'll know that you will always respect the written word. You will never insult the reader of your email with misspelled words or bad grammar. And by doing so, you will show your respect for them.

When you write an email, remember also that adjectives are little editorials. Use them sparingly. After all, what does terrific really mean? Was the proposal really fabulous? Was the meeting really wonderful? Avoid meaningless words such as "very." If you say someone is very considerate, how much more considerate is he or she? These words may work well in conversation, but in email, we're creating a new way to speak. We are talking in e-speak.

We hope this book helped you in answering those tricky questions about the most fun and fastest growing form of communication today. From happy hour announcements to corporate memos, comprehensive email instruction can lend a hand to us all.

Can I send large attachments over email?

Do not send huge attachments by email to mass email lists or even to individuals, without asking your recipients if they can open them. Although networks are getting faster all the time, for now it is important to ask your recipient how much his or her network can handle. A download time of 20 minutes drains company resources and the recipient's patience. Also, some Internet service providers (ISPs) place a limit on the size of any individual email message that can be handled on their email servers.

We also hope this book dispels some myths about email communication (it's okay to email a thank you message to your boss) while preserving others (yes, you should always use an appropriate subject header, greeting, and closing in emails).

If you have some email horror stories or tips you would like to share with us, please visit our Web site. We are looking for new stories for our sequel. Our Web address is: www.dontstubyourpinkie.com

Thank you! In closing we have just a few things to say.

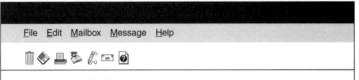

File   Edit   Mailbox   Message   Help

Dear Email Champions,

Take heed friends. Now you have a chance to show the *true you* in your emails. By following the information we've provided in this book, you will be respected in a whole new way. And please, never send a dull email!

Don't stub your pinkie on the space bar and keep clicking!

Your friends,
Maureen and Sandy

PS Until next time!

EMAIL TERMS AND SYMBOLS

A few frequently used emoticons (view them sideways):

:-), :) **Smile.**

;-) **Wink and a smile.**

:-o **Oh, my gosh! Astonishment.**

:-(**Sad, frown. Might help with delivering sad news.**

: > **Half smile.**

For more emoticons, please refer to www.aol.com and go to Keyword: LOL online.

Useful Terms

Emailers: Email users.

Mass Email: An email sent to a large list of recipients.

Emoticon: A symbol used in email to convey an emotion, such as anger, happiness, etc.

Cling-ons: Emailers who won't stop emailing someone, especially forwarded emails.

Snail Mail: Letter sent the old-fashioned way—through the regular mail.

Web: World Wide Web.

Everyone Rule: When sending an email, assume that everyone and anyone you know or don't know can read your email. Before sending your email, consider that your grandmother, priest or rabbi, children, boss, and even the government will read this email. Police yourself with this rule and avoid embarrassment. When in doubt, do without.

Acknowledgment: A quick and courteous email sent to let the sender know that you have received his or her email.

Trojan horse: A computer virus that appears innocuous but, once within your system, will wreak havoc. Named for the Trojan horse the Greeks used to penetrate the walls of Troy.

Email Acronyms

Classic acronyms, common in business settings:

COB   Close of Business

FYI   For Your Information

BTW   By the Way

FWIW   For What It's Worth

WWW   World Wide Web or the Web

Casual acronyms, used in informal emails:

LOL   Laughing out loud

IMHO   In my humble opinion

THE BASICS OF EMAILING

We have created a list of the most common features on your email. Before using email, you may consider the following tips. Or, just brush up on them if you are a more experienced emailer.

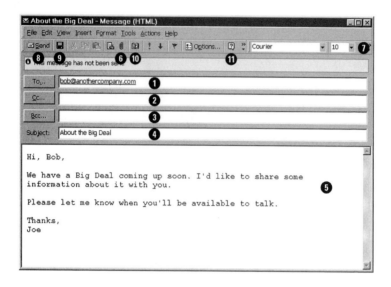

1. To

This line requires you to enter the email address of the person or persons to whom you are sending the email.

2. CC or Copy

You can copy your email to others, just as you would copy a memo to others. CC stands for carbon copy.

3. BCC or Blind Carbon Copy

Enter the addresses of the persons to whom you would like this email blind copied. In other words, no other recipient knows who else received the email. This option is used most often for mailing lists. Use it when you would like to send an email to a group of people without having recipients know the identity of the other recipients.

4. Subject/Topic

Enter the subject of your email here. It is important to use a subject header so that your recipient can know, at a glance in his or her inbox, what the email is about. Clear subject headers will help your recipient in prioritizing messages.

5. Writing Space

You may type the message of your email into the writing space as you would fill up the page on a typewriter. At the end of a line, most email programs return automatically, so you do not need to do that manually.

6. Attachments

In addition to the written message you send to your recipient, you may attach an electronic document as well, for instance, a spreadsheet, a digital photograph, or a letter written in a word processing application. When you click on the attachments icon (usually depicted by a paper clip or other icon that denotes "attached files"), you will be directed to the file directory on your computer, and may choose the file you would like to attach to the email.

7. Toolbar/Power Bar

Many email programs have "toolbars," or a bar featuring many frequently used icons, at the top of the screen. The icons help users find and use the program's various options more easily.

Possible features of the toolbar:

→ Font—choose the font you would like to use (Times New Roman, etc.)

→ Font size—choose the point size (10 or 12 point. Please, nothing smaller than that.)

→ Bold

→ Underline

→ Italics

→ Color

Other options:

→ Spell check

→ Information, help, etc.

Some of the feature options are only useful if you are sending emails to others who have the same software packages. For example, if you have AOL, and are sending a fellow AOL subscriber an email, then the features such as bold, color, and italics will take effect. If you are sending an AOL email to a Lotus Notes user, for example, these features will not transmit. You will simply have a "text" email, which is text only, and without any formatting.

8. Send

Click on send when you have completed your email. The email will be sent to the recipient or recipients.

9. Saving Emails Before Sending Or Send Later

It is possible to save your email before you send it. Maybe you would like some time to think about your email before sending. Perhaps you need some further information that is not at your fingertips to complete the email. To retrieve your saved message, check your email file cabinet or outgoing mailbox.

10. Address Book

An address book in which you can enter names and email addresses is a common software package feature. When you would like to retrieve an address, open the address book and look up the name of the person you wish to send the email to. You can also save group lists in your email address book. These will come in handy for mail merged letters. Once in the address book, you can search for "lists" or some equivalent feature that will allow you to create a group list. You can even name your group list so it is easy to remember and retrieve.

When using AOL, for example, here are the steps to creating a mailing list, as found under HELP/Mail/Creating mailing lists:

1. Click on the Mail Center icon on the toolbar and select Address Book from the menu.

2. Click New Group.

3. In the Group Name field, type the name you will use to refer to this mailing list.
   For example: My online friends

4. In the Addresses field, type the screen names and/or Internet email addresses of the people you want to include on this mailing list, separating each name with a comma.
   For example: AOLMember1, name@companyname.com, AOLMember2

(© Copyright 1995–1998 America Online, Inc. All Rights Reserved.)

11. Help

Always there to save the day, the help option generally has a long index of topics from which to choose. Some email programs have a search vehicle, which allows you to key in the subject of your question or area of concern and then finds the solution, information, or instructions that you are looking for. If the help index and accompanying instructions are not able to help you, call your system administrator or software provider for further assistance.

Other Features

Templates

Templates are an important feature for people who tend to email many "form" letters. There are several ways to save your template. We will use AOL as our first example and Microsoft Outlook as our second.

AOL Templates

→ One way to create a template is by saving the letter in a file in your word processing program, retrieving it when needed, copying it, and pasting it into your email.

→ Or, you can actually attach a document in its entirety to your email. Located on the bottom of the WRITE MAIL screen is ATTACHMENTS. Click on this and click on ATTACH and your computer directory will be shown.

→ Access your word processing documents, select the document you would like to attach, and then click on OK. Your document will be attached to your email.

→ Or, create a template within your email program. Click on WRITE and then compose your email, the text of which will be your "form letter" for storage. To save the email, the Address space must be filled, so for now, use your own address. (When you bring up the letter to use later, change the address line to reflect the recipient's address or the name of the group email list. Make sure to clearly denote the subject of the email in the header, for example, "Fund-raising letter," so you know which of the templates it is. Once finished with the email, click on SEND LATER instead of send, in order to store the document. The message will be saved in your Message Waiting to Be Sent file of your Personal Filing Cabinet located under My Files. This is also called your offline mailbox. Each time you go onto AOL after saving this document, a message will flash in your screen telling you about your stored mail. Click on SEND LATER.

→ When you would like to retrieve this letter, access the Message Waiting to Be Sent file, and click on your email template. The email will be set up ready to go. Remember to change the To space from your name to the name of the email recipient.

Microsoft Outlook Template

For our second example, we will use Microsoft Outlook to give you an idea of how to use templates:

→ Open the item you want to save as a template or create a new one.

→ On the File menu, click Save As when you are ready to save the template.

→ In the File name box, type a name for the file.

→ In the Save As type box, click Outlook Template.

→ In the Save box, click the location where you want to save the file.

→ If you save a template in the Outlook folder, the template appears on the Outlook tab when you point to New and on the File menu and then click Choose Template. If you save the template in another folder, it does not appear in the Outlook tab.

Mail Merge

If you would like to mail your template or any other email to a group of people, seek out the mail merge feature on your email system if available. We will look at AOL again for our first example.

➔ First, create an email you would like to be your template, or access a stored template in your system. Or access a word processing document and cut and paste the contents into the COMPOSE area of the screen, where you do the writing.

➔ Then, insert your email address in the TO space. You will be sending this email to yourself, and everyone else. Retrieve your group list from your address book. Place the group list in your BCC screen. Remember the rule on mass emails—do not send unsolicited mass emails, and if you do, then send the email in such a way that the recipients do not get a long list of everyone on your group email list. (If you insert the group list into the TO space, your email will not be sent privately to the recipients. All email addresses in that list will appear to every one of the recipients.) By placing the list in the BCC line, you are protecting the privacy of the people on your email list.

➔ Once you have the letter in place, and the email addresses in BCC, you may click SEND and your mail merge is on its way. Each recipient will receive your email in his or her mailbox. Once the recipient opens the mail, he or she will see your message, and see that it was from you, but also *to* you. No other names are mentioned in the address fields. Your BCC address list carried out its job.

For our second example, we will take another look at MS Outlook:

→ If you use Microsoft Word, you can use the Outlook contact list as a data source for a mail merge in Word to produce a variety of merged documents. For example, you can create form letters, print a list of mailing labels, or print addresses on envelopes.

→ There are two ways to use the Outlook contact list as a mail merge data source in Word, based on the fields you want available in Word. The contact list can be in a private or public folder.

→ Use a contact list in the Outlook Address Book if you want to use standard name, address, and phone number fields for Outlook contacts in Word. Use Outlook contacts as a mail merge data source in Word.

→ Use an exported Outlook contact list if you want to use any field in the complete list of fields, except custom fields, in Word. Also use this method if you use Word 95.

Return Receipt

These are not just available at your local post office. Return receipt is alive and well in your email software program. Would you like to know when your recipient received your email? (Meaning, not just when the email lands in his or her online mailbox, but when the recipient actually *open*s the email.) Return receipt on email is similar to its counterpart in the postal service. You can get written notification that your recipient has retrieved your message, but you can't always guarantee that the person has *read* your email.

Sometimes, with all of the emails that people receive these days, they might click open your email, but then get distracted by something else and not read it. In any case, once your recipient has retrieved the message, an instant message will be relayed back to you detailing the date and time that your email regarding (subject) has been received by recipient (name). Another related option, if available, is to simply receive the delivery time of the email, which might be enough for some users.

Organizing Messages

Your online mailbox has dozens of new email messages. How do you begin to tackle the emails—the order in which they were received? Or by importance? Or eeny-meeny-miney-mo? Keep in mind the following pointers when sorting through your emails.

→ Open urgent emails first. Emails labeled "urgent," "time sensitive," "respond immediately," or something to that effect clearly demand your immediate attention. Respond to these emails before handling any others.

→ Open emails from clients, the boss, a fellow team member, the system administrator, or other important people as soon as possible. These people may send urgent emails but may not label them as such. Or, their emails might include information that you need to know. Respond to the emails that need your immediate attention.

→ Are there certain people whose emails you enjoy? Read them next. Maybe the colleague in the room next to you has a flair for writing interesting emails. Why save the good ones for last?

→ Read emails from others *you know*. Delete any emails with suspicious attachments. (See chapter 15 for more information on attachments and viruses.) Look at the emails from addresses *you do not know*. Are there any suspicious messages with strange attachments inside? Delete these.

→ Or, you may discover emails from people you do not know, without an attachment or any other suspicious information. You may open these. You may find one of them is an email from your boss's florist, telling you to expect a surprise at about 4 p.m. Aren't you glad you opened that one?

→ Acknowledge emails that need acknowledgment. Thank a person for his or her email. Respond to a request. Do not leave the sender hanging. Or email the sender and let him or her know when you will give the email your attention, should it need follow-up. If someone sends you an email that doesn't need a reply, then don't. If someone thanks you for your thank you note, for instance, stop right there.

→ Cleaning. If you have read an email and want to address it later, save the file and it will remain in your online mailbox. Save important emails in your email "filing cabinet" if you would like to save them. Perhaps the email applies to a client with whom you are working. You have a file on that client in your cabinet and you want to save it there. Or, the email can be used as a record of proof for an official situation. Lastly, delete emails that you do not want, to free up space on your system. Once every week, delete your deleted files. Do not forget about them.

Think of a deleted email as you would garbage: When you delete it, it goes in the trash. When you delete the deleted email, you are taking out the trash.

→ Review your emails one more time. Answer all of them if you are able to at that time, and take care of issues that need your attention. Try to tackle the emails at one time, or they will pile up on you. If you do not wish to tackle some of the unimportant emails, then you might want a backup reminder, either through your computer system or written on a piece of paper. With so many emails to handle, it is easy to forget to answer all of them.

Email Software

There are quite a few email software programs available, from stand-alone programs to shareware or freeware versions to programs integrated into Web browsers. There are also all kinds of add-ons and specialized software programs available that perform nifty tasks such as message notification, spam screening, converting email to voice messages, synchronizing address books, virus checking, and message encrypting, to name a few.

Most of the leading email programs are fairly similar in their features and capabilities. Chances are, you are already using one of these, so there is little reason to change programs. They all offer features such as filtering, message searching, organizing messages in folders, multiple address books, and attaching files. The following are some of the leading email software programs (listed alphabetically so we don't get anyone mad at us):

Company	Software	Web Site
America Online	AOL Mail	www.aol.com
Micro Computer Systems	Calypso	www.mcsdallas.com
Lotus	CC:Mail	www.lotus.com
Qualcomm	Eudora	www.eudora.com
Novell	GroupWise	www.novell.com
Netscape	Messenger	www.netscape.com
Microsoft	Outlook Express	www.microsoft.com
David Harris	Pegasus Mail	www.pegasus.usa.com
Commtouch	Prontomail	www.prontomail.com
CE Software	QuickMail	www.cesoft.com
Teamware	Teamware Office	www.teamware.com
NetManage	Z-Mail for Unix	www.netmanage.com

For information about all the various specialized and add-on email software products available, try: http://everythingemail.net.

For information about various bulk email software packages, check out: www.vome.com.

Index